The Doctrine of the Shape of the Earth:

A Comprehensive Biblical Perspective

Written By: Nathan Roberts

The Doctrine of the Shape of the Earth

Paperback Book ISBN: 978-1-549900-10-5

nathan@FlatEarthDoctrine.com

www.FlatEarthDoctrine.com

TABLE OF CONTENTS

INTRODUCTION

When I first heard debates about the shape of the Earth, I initially reflected with these sentiments:

"What does it matter?"

"I'm not stupid! There is no way I've believed a lie about such a fundamental aspect of my existence."

"Who would manufacture such a silly lie, and for what seemingly inconsequential gain?"

"How can anyone know?"

As I began studying God's Word, which I have found corroborates precisely with our reality, the answers to my many questions became clear. And, I quickly realized why the doctrine of the shape of the Earth is important to all, not just the Christian. The heart of this book is to encourage two groups of people:

1st The Christian: Once a man wholeheartedly embraces God's Word (manifested as Jesus Christ; John 1:1) as Faithful and True, only then will he live a life that shouts no hope or truth exists that is contrary to God's Word. Only then will the prayers of believers in Yeshua (Hebrew word for "Jesus") HaMashiac (Hebrew word for "the Messiah") become more relevant, frequent and fervent, and as a result, more powerful and effective. Their zeal for the Great Commission is enriched (Matthew 28:16-20).

<u>2nd The Non-Christian:</u> When a man comes face-to-face with the reality that the Flat Earth is scientific truth and it agrees with the Bible, his strong resistance towards the God of the Bible begins to disintegrate. He becomes open to the possibility that the God of the Bible has offered him a remedy for his sin through a repentant heart and faith in His only begotten Son, Yeshua, as his Lord and Savior.

The chapter titled "Truth Leads to Yeshua" is dedicated to testimonies that bare witness to the impact that the doctrine of the shape of the Earth has already had, and will continue to have, in many lives.

Something else I have learned on my journey in the doctrine of the shape of the Earth is that the words of God and his character are compared to the likeness of His Earth, making this topic even that much more important for us to better understand our God through His creation. I will share even more examples throughout this book, however, here is just one powerful example.

Psalm 119:89-90 from the Amplified Cross Reference Bible states: "Forever, O Lord, Your word is settled in heaven [stands firm as the heavens]. Your faithfulness is from generation to generation; You have established the earth, and it stands fast."

What does it mean to have "...established the earth, and it stands fast."?

The Merriam-Webster Dictionary defines the word "establish" as:

1. to institute permanently

2. to make firm or stable

3. to put a firm basis.

The word "stand" is defined as:

1. to take or be at rest in an upright or firm position

2. to assume a specified position

3. to remain stationary or unchanged

4. to be steadfast

5. to set upright

6. to oppose or resist change.

The word "fast" is defined to mean "in a firm or fixed manner."

Using the descriptions for the words in this
passage, it is quite clear to see that God's
faithfulness is being compared to the Earth which is
stable, fixed, firm, remains stationary, steadfast,
unchanged, instituted permanently, that is set
upright and opposes or resists change. Psalms
119:89-90 contains a parallel as to how God
expects us to believe upon His faithfulness just as
surely as we live upon His created Earth that is
stationary, stable, set upright and fixed beneath
our feet.

As a firm believer in Yeshua as my redeemer and
someone who relies on God's Word as the
authority for my life, I naturally have a deep desire
to understand God's perspective on everything,
including the shape of the Earth. After spending
many hours researching God's Word, praying for
wisdom and discernment, and performing scientific
experiments I humbly and gratefully submit my
findings to you.

Before you move onto the next chapter titled "My
Flat Earth Story," please take the time to read the
following passage because it serves as just another
testament as to why men, women, and children are
so lost and without hope when they do not
wholeheartedly trust in God's Word. I hope you
can see the connection between the following

passage and the doctrine of the shape of the Earth, as you read along.

"Because that which may be known of Elohim is manifest in them; for Elohim hath shewed it unto them. For the invisible things of him from the creation of the world are clearly seen, being understood by the things that are made, even his eternal power and Majesty; so that they are without excuse: Because that, when they knew Elohim, they glorified him not as Elohim, neither were thankful; but became vain in their imaginations, and their foolish heart was darkened. Professing themselves to be wise, they became fools, And changed the glory of the uncorruptible Elohim into an image made like to corruptible man, and to birds, and fourfooted beasts, and creeping things. Wherefore Elohim also gave them up to uncleanness through the lusts of their own hearts, to dishonour their own bodies between themselves: Who changed the truth of Elohim into a lie, and worshipped and served the creature more than the Creator, who is blessed for ever. Amen. For this cause Elohim gave them up unto vile affections: for even their women did change the natural use into that which is against nature: And likewise also the men, leaving the natural use of the woman, burned in their lust one toward another; men with men working that which is unseemly, and receiving in themselves that recompence of their error which was meet. And even as they did not like to retain Elohim in their knowledge, Elohim gave them over to a reprobate mind, to do those things which are not convenient; Being filled with all unrighteousness, fornication, wickedness, covetousness, maliciousness; full of envy, murder, debate, deceit, malignity; whisperers, Backbiters, haters of Elohim, despiteful, proud, boasters, inventors of evil things, disobedient to parents, Without understanding, covenantbreakers, without natural affection, implacable, unmerciful: Who knowing the judgment of Elohim, that they which commit such things are worthy of death, not only do the same, but have pleasure in them that do them." - Romans 1:19-32 (Restoration Study Bible)

CHAPTER 1: MY FLAT EARTH STORY

By now, you likely are wondering, "What happened in this man's life that led him to spend so much time on the doctrine of the shape of the Earth that he has enough content to write this book?"

Well, it was spring of 2015, and I was scrolling through my Facebook newsfeed and saw a ridiculous video posted. The video was of a Saudi cleric attempting to explain that the way a plane can fly over Earth without any account for the alleged spin of the Earth should be considered a proof that the Earth is stationary. [a]

Sheikh Bandar Al-Khaybari, a Saudi cleric, proclaims on MEMRI TV on January 2015 that the Earth does not spin. He stated that airplanes would be able to arrive at destinations to their west by basically hovering above the ground because the Earth beneath should be spinning to the east thereby naturally bringing lands to the west nearer. Furthermore, he also stated that airplanes going eastward would not be able to arrive at their destinations to the east because the spin of the Earth (west to east) is at a faster speed than an average airplane travels.

That was my first encounter where the globular shaped spinning Earth was ever challenged. Of course, my instincts quickly kicked in, and I unashamedly ridiculed, mocked and laughed at the thought that someone believed what we'd been told about the Earth by all the governments on the Earth to be false. I was too busy laughing even to take time to consider the Saudi cleric's point that the spin of the Earth, should it exist, would have to be taken into account for every aircraft lift-off, flight path, travel time, and aircraft landing, although, it is not. Perhaps, I should have listened. Because I didn't listen, I experienced the folly and shame as described in Proverbs 18:13 which is translated from the King James Version Bible as: "He that answereth a matter before he heareth it, it is folly and shame unto him."

Several months later, December 2015, what I thought the shape of the Earth to be was challenged yet again. This time it was by an author, David E. Robinson, who knows the Bible very well and is a self-avowed Christian. If I recall correctly, he posted on his blog a picture taken of the Alaskan horizon, which was obviously flat, and made a matter of fact statement to the effect of, "Well if this doesn't prove the Earth is flat, I don't know what does!" And I have since tried to find that blog post but do not see it, though he still has plenty of Flat Earth related posts. [b]

Perhaps, I chuckled a bit, though I didn't laugh this time. I was extremely puzzled because this was a man who I had grown to respect and could not simply laugh him off without reasonable cause.

Now, I had to dig in and research this nonsensical stationary Flat Earth "theory" and debunk it so I could move on in my life with more important topics worthy of my time to study.

After six months of attempting to prove I was living on a globe shaped Earth spinning on its axis at approximately 1,080 mph while orbiting the Sun at a mean velocity of 66,600 mph while the solar system orbits around the Milky Way at approximately 420,000 mph while the Milky Way itself is ripping through the galaxy at a trajectory of approximately 2,237,000 mph, I failed. Even when I tried to solve this mystery with the standard answer of "gravity," much to my dismay, I realized gravity is simply a theory and not a fact. For something to be a "fact" it must be something that is indisputably the case, and gravity is NOT indisputable.

If "Gravity" were this amazingly powerful thing that makes you and everything else on this Earth stick to the Earth, how come you can watch smoke from a fire rise and a helium balloon float up? Shouldn't gravity be holding these things down to the Earth? Why is it that you can watch a bee or a gnat effortlessly flying in the air defying "gravity," has it achieved "zero gravity?"

The real answer to these "phenomena" is much more basic and simpler than you may even guess. The answer is, density. Things that are lighter than air, or that can use the wind to glide, will rise. Things being heavier than air, or are not using the wind to glide, will fall.

In water, it is buoyancy that must be taken into account. This is why air bubbles beneath the water rise, and why a rock beneath the water will go to the bottom.

You can test it for yourself in the pool. Fill your lungs with air, and you should likely float. Of course, all is proportionate to your weight and the amount of air your lungs can hold. Then, blow out all the air from your lungs, and you should notice yourself beginning to sink.

Now, if you are seeking for me to provide you with a citation or reference from a professional "Scientist" who has written a book or scientific journal that agrees with my assessment, you shouldn't hold your breath. You will have to learn to trust your God-given senses, and I will elaborate on this very point throughout.

In any case, I found zero evidence for the ludicrous speeds postulated by the Heliocentric Universe model, as well as, many other contradictions for the "Science" claims of a globular shaped spinning Earth. And when I say "Science" (capital "S"), that is referring to pseudo-science vs. "science" (lower case "s") that is real science. And until my investigation into the Flat Earth, I did not know there to be a difference.

Merriam-Webster Dictionary defines the word "science" as:

1) the state of knowing: knowledge as distinguished from ignorance or misunderstanding

2) knowledge about or study of the natural world based on facts learned through experiments and observation

In short, Merriam-Webster Dictionary defines "science" as "knowledge." If you do NOT have "knowledge," then you lack "science." "Science" and "knowledge" are the same thing. Whenever a

Christian says, "The Bible is not a book of science." Little do they know the ignorance they have just revealed in themselves, for what they have just said is that the Bible is not a book of knowledge.

I have witnessed too many people in the "Mainstream Christian Community" who have a large following, such as, David Platt, the founder of Secret Church, who have openly mocked and bashed the Biblically based stationary and Flat Earth. David Platt and many others claim the Bible is not a book of "Science." True, it is NOT a book of "Science," with a capital "S," because that is a type of religion that blindly follows worldly and unsubstantiated claims in favor of actual "science" with a lower case "s." The Bible is a book of many things, including a book of "knowledge." If you do not think so, you may think differently after reading only the thirty-one chapters in the book of Proverbs, let alone many other books of the Bible.

As for me, what I found after gaining knowledge, Biblical and experiential, about my natural world based on facts learned through my experiments, and my observations are that a globe shaped Earth is pseudo-science. Which may have been a similar battle Paul was trying to convey to Timothy when he wrote warning him in 1 Timothy 6:20 to avoid "...science falsely so called:" This section of scripture could have just as well have been interpreted as "knowledge falsely so called." "Modern Science" tells us that Earth was created from a Big Bang without God, and we evolved from monkeys. Unfortunately, many so-called Christians do not challenge these claims, and in some cases fully embrace them.

According to Ecclesiastes 1:9, there is "...nothing new under the sun." Is it possible that the early saints had to combat the same type of heresies within their congregation? Maybe? Just maybe?

In any case, I have concluded that much in the same way many a man has set upon the course to debunk the existence and deity of our Lord and Savior, Yeshua, so it is for those who earnestly, not flippantly, attempt to debunk a stationary and flat shaped Earth. My goal is not to prove anything to you, as that is impossible to prove something for someone. It is the responsibility of each observer to determine if a "proof" actually proves anything. You must become the observer, and while reading books like this are helpful, I encourage you to research beyond this book. And most importantly, your eyes will not see what your mind will not permit, so please prepare to open your mind to God's Word. And, as 1 Thessalonians 5:21 encourages us to "Prove all things; hold fast that which is good."

CHAPTER 2: EARTH SHAPE MODELS

While this may seem to be a very elementary topic, I feel it necessary to establish with as few words as possible very clearly the differences between the two primary Earth shape models that are promulgated, and that being the Globe Earth and the Flat Earth. Each is an interesting concept. However, it is a logical fallacy for both to be considered the truth of our reality while remaining consistent with God's Word, as they are each unique to themselves.

What matters most, and will be the focus throughout this book, is seeking what is written in God's Word about the shape of the Earth. So, let us take a glance at the main premises for each of these two Earth shape models.

GLOBE EARTH

The Globe Earth proposes the shape of the Earth to be a perfectly shaped ball and at the very least an oblate spheroid. The Globe Earth can exist in either a Heliocentric Universe where the Sun is the center of the universe and the Earth orbits the Sun, or it can exist in a Geocentric Universe where the Globe Earth is the center of the universe, and the Sun orbits the Earth. Thus, a Globe Earth may or may not spin. Though the most unifying aspects of a Globe Earth model is that:

The Doctrine of the Shape of the Earth

1. At sea level the surface of the Earth curves downward from the observer in every direction and naturally impossible for anything to be level over any distance, much less a vast distance, when using a true leveling tool. (Please, note the word "level" in "sea level." "Level" means having a flat and even surface without slopes or bumps.)

2. Water from the oceans, lakes, and rivers must stick to the Earth and curve around the sphere.

3. A magical force called "gravity," which is outside of the naturally known elements must exist to keep most objects toward the ground to justify why nothing slides off the Earth's curvature and flies into the Earth's atmosphere.

NASA image named Blue Marble West. HINT: Look up the legal definition of the word "image" as you will find the word "photo" is nowhere to be found because it's NOT a photo! It's CGI (computer-generated image), a composite. There is NOT 1 real picture that exists which shows the full earth from one side of the alleged globe.

FLAT EARTH

The Flat Earth is quite simple in comparison to the Globe Earth. The Earth beneath one's feet on the Flat Earth is immovable, stationary, and a fixed plane where the outer most southern edges are Antarctica with a dome (aka firmament) overhead. The "edges" of the Earth are where the dome meets the Antarctica land mass. On a Flat Earth there exist hills, mountains, and valleys, however, sea *level* always maintains true level throughout the Earth. And density/buoyancy is what determines whether something rises or falls.

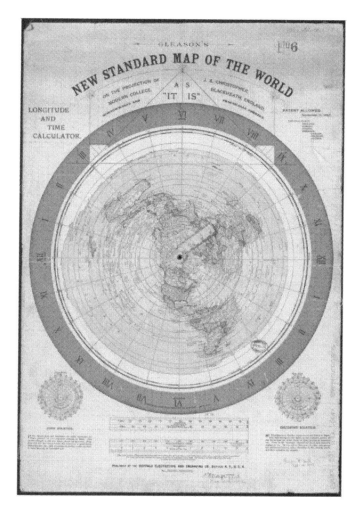

Azimuthal Equidistant map patented by Alexander Gleason in 1892.

CHAPTER 3: WORLDLY VS. BIBLICAL PERSPECTIVE OF EARTH

Is it even possible that the entire world could be deceived? Biblically speaking, yes it is. Let's take a look at the following passage from the Restoration Study Bible.

"And the great dragon was cast out, that old serpent, called the Devil, and Satan, which **deceiveth the whole world**..." - Revelation 12:9

Fortunately, one day, the one who deceives the whole world will be locked up so the nations will be deceived no more.

"And cast him into the bottomless pit, and shut him up, and set a seal upon him, that **he should deceive the nations no more**..." - Revelation 20:3

Even some who deny the relevancy of the Bible in their own life will readily admit that the books contained in the Bible (including 1 Enoch) point to a geocentric Flat Earth universe model. Matt Boylan (aka Powerland), Eric Dubay, and Mark Sargent have been on the forefront of raising awareness to the true nature and geometric shape of the Earth, and each makes reference to the Bible. Unfortunately, at least to my knowledge, none proclaims to believe in Yeshua as their Lord and Savior.

Just as unfortunate, still today many self-proclaimed Bible believers when confronted with the truth about the shape of the Earth from an entirely Biblical perspective choose to ignore or dismiss it. Instead, they continue to live in denial of this Biblically based doctrine while willingly replacing it with a worldly based doctrine, or choose neither doctrine and unnecessarily flounder when they could stand firmly on God's Word just as surely as they believe in Yeshua as their Savior. It is truly heartbreaking when the Holy Scriptures could not be any clearer on a particular topic, and self-proclaimed Bible believers still choose NOT to stand firmly on God's Word.

Yes, I refer to the shape of the Earth as a Biblical doctrine; though please do not confuse my use of the term Biblical doctrine as automatically being associated with a salvation issue. I do not view the doctrine of the shape of the Earth to be in it of itself a salvation issue. Though for many this doctrine has become a stumbling block and can rob us of a closer relationship with Yeshua (aka the manifested Word of God; John 1:1-5) due to a lack of confidence and trust in God's Word.

What is "doctrine?" The Merriam-Webster Dictionary defines the word doctrine as "something that is taught." That is it. So, if it is something that is taught, then it may be appropriately referred to as a doctrine. The books contained in the Bible teach on the shape of the Earth. Therefore, it is appropriate to classify, without any hesitation, that the shape of the Earth is, in fact, a Biblical doctrine.

And, while you may still be somewhat skeptical of what you are reading, I am sure that if you are a Christian then we can at least find common ground through one particular Bible passage.

"All scripture is given by inspiration of God, and is ***profitable for doctrine, for reproof, for correction,*** for instruction in righteousness: That the man of God may be perfect thoroughly furnished unto all good works." - 2 Timothy 3:16-17 (KJV)

I have discovered in my life that the times when I have half-heartedly believed in God's Word, it fractured my faith in God. Faith is our salvation, that being faith in Yeshua. By NOT accepting the entire Bible to be "Faithful and True" eventually leads to a lukewarm faith, or even worse a denial that Yeshua is Lord and Savior. Sound Biblical doctrine is essential to living an abundant and productive life for God.

I firmly believe that the true premise of the satanically based Heliocentric Universe model is to delude one's faith in God's Word by attacking our subconscious. Because, think of how many atheists have reasoned, "If God does not know how to adequately describe the Earth in His 'Flawless & Holy Scriptures' that He supposedly created, then how can I trust He created it? Much less, trust Him with my life?" And for the Christian who has reasoned (this was me), "Well, Christ did die on the cross for my sins, though much of the Bible is poetry and metaphors so the Bible can't be that relevant to my everyday life. I mean, even the authors of God's Word didn't understand what we now know about Science. So not everything in the Bible is spot on."

Yeshua is referred to as being called "Faithful and True" in Revelation 19:11 when he returns to bring righteous judgment to the Earth. The word "Faithful" is Strong's Greek Dictionary #4103 and is defined as objectively, trustworthy; subjectively, trustful:--believe(-ing, -r), faithful(-ly), sure, true. The word "True" is Strong's Greek Dictionary #228 and is defined as: truthful:--true.

Do you trust Jesus Christ, the manifested Word of God (John 1:1), who will return as Faithful and True?

Throughout this book, I will challenge you to ask yourself the following question: "Do I believe all of God's Word to be Faithful and True?"

Now, let's dive into seventeen well-documented topics in the Bible related to our physical reality, so that according to Exodus 9:29 (RSB) "...that thou mayest know how that the Earth is Yahweh's."

ORDER OF CREATION

Have you ever built a house, or at the very least do you understand the fundamentals of building a house? If so, do you know when building the house what should be built first? That's right, the foundation. Once the foundation is established, then everything else can be constructed in its proper order upon that foundation to eventually create the finished house.

Who first modeled the principle of building the foundation first? That's right; God did it during the creation of His Earth.

Let us examine the order of creation as stated in Genesis:

1st Day) The heaven, Earth, dark and light was created. (Genesis 1:1-5)

2nd Day) The firmament was created to divide the waters under the firmament from the waters above the firmament. (Genesis 1:6-8)

3rd Day) Dry land (aka Earth), waters (aka Sea), grass, herb-yielding seed, and fruit were created. (Genesis 1:9-13)

4th Day) Two lights were placed in the heaven; the *Sun* to rule the day and Moon to rule the night, and He created the stars, to be for signs, and for seasons, and for days, and years. (Genesis 1:14-19)

5th Day) Creatures of the water and fowl that fly above the Earth in the open firmament heaven were created. (Genesis 1:20-23)

6th Day) The Earth brings forth living creatures, cattle, and creeping things and beast of the Earth. Man (male/female) is created in God's image to be fruitful and multiply and to have dominion over all living creatures. (Genesis 1:24-31)

7th Day) The heavens and the Earth were finished, and all the host of them, and God ended his work and rested. (Genesis 2:1-3)

The Earth was created on the first day and the Sun was created on the fourth day. Why did God create the Earth before the Sun? It stands to reason that the God of order created in order by creating the foundation first. The Earth is the foundation of the universe, and as such, it had to be established before the Sun, Moon, and everything else. If the Sun were the center of our universe, then it would stand to reason that the Sun would have been created first, though it was not so according to God's Word.

Just as a man builds a house beginning with its foundation, so it was when God created the heavens, Earth and the host of them. He first made the foundation, the Earth, and then He made all the supporting elements. From a Biblical perspective the Sun is not the center of the universe; rather, it is the Earth that is the center of the universe.

Though, let's entertain the idea that God created His Earth to be a globe shape. What was the Globe Earth orbiting around for 3 days until the Sun was created?

Another thing that I would like to bring to your attention while we are on the topic of the general universe is just one more clear contradiction between what the world claims and what the Word of God states. Genesis 2:1 states, "Thus the heavens and the Earth were finished, and all the host of them." When God created the heavens, Earth, and hosts, thereof, it was finished back in Genesis. All the hosts of heaven, meaning Sun, Moon, and stars, were finished and no more hosts needed to be created because it was ***finished***.

So, the proclamation by the "Scientific Communities" that the universe is infinitely expanding at an exponential rate is a direct contradiction to Biblical truth. The Word of God does not support, or even suggest, an ever-expanding universe, rather, just the opposite.

"Thus the heavens and the Earth were finished, and all the host of them." - Genesis 2:1 (Restoration Study Bible)

There is a proper order for building, as prescribed throughout God's creation, and quality home builders follow the Creator's established principle, too, by first building the foundation. For the construction of our universe, from a Biblical perspective, the foundation is the Earth, not the Sun.

Do you boldly believe all of God's Word to be Faithful and True?

MEASUREMENTS

"Where wast thou when I laid the foundations of the earth? Declare, if thou hast understanding. Who hath laid the measures thereof, if thou knowest?" - Job 38:4-5 (Restoration Study Bible)

NASA and the scientific community have convinced the public that they have already accomplished everything that could be discovered and known about the dimensions of Earth. This includes the measurements of the Earth; above ground, below the ground, and everything in between.

The globular shaped Earth reportedly has a circumference of approximately 24,901 miles. The Earth's radius is allegedly 3,963 miles. That sure is a lot of Earth beneath our feet, which should require extensive exploration and research before defining, labeling, and educating the public of its characteristics, agreed?

Well, according to the scientific community every layer of the Earth has been discovered and defined all the way to the core of the Earth. The USGS (United States Geological Survey) tells the public that there are primarily three layers of the Earth. The crust is the top surface of the Earth with a reported depth that ranges between 0 and 62 miles. Just below the crust is the mantle with a reported depth that spans between 62 miles and 1,801 miles from the top-most part of the crust. Lastly, the core of the Earth allegedly spans between 1,801 miles and 3,963 miles from the top-most part of the crust.

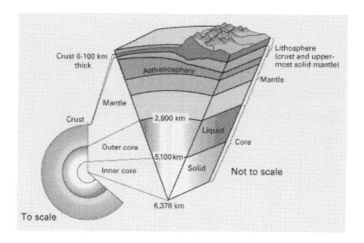

USGS (https://pubs.usgs.gov/gip/dynamic/inside.html)

How do we know that these are the actual layers of the Earth? Who went there to verify? How was it accomplished, and when?

What do you believe to be the furthest depths to the core of the Earth that man has ever gone? 50 miles? 200 miles? Not even close.

The furthest man has documented drilling into the Earth is only approximately 7.5 miles with the Kola Superdeep Borehole.[c] It took place in 1989 at Kola Peninsula, Russia. They allegedly were unable to drill any further due to the heat of the Earth's core. Also, keep in mind that distance of 7.5 miles is how far the drill was documented as drilling down, and not the distance that a man went down into the Earth's crust.

Whatever the actual reason for the Kola Superdeep
Borehole being unable to drill past 7.5 miles is
inconsequential. What matters most is that what
government agencies and every text book in the
public and private schools has recorded about the
layers of the Earth versus what has been
experienced is a laughable discrepancy. In fact, the
discrepancy between what the public has been told
and what has been explored is only a minuscule
difference of 3,955.5 miles (3,963-7.5). And it is
about the same as man's exploration of the depths
of the sea.

On March 26, 2012, James Cameron reached the
bottom of the Challenger Deep, the deepest part of
the Mariana Trench, at a record setting 35,787 feet
(6.77 miles) below sea level.[d] As impressive as it
may sound being that it is a "record," it is still a
laughable discrepancy between what the public has
been told versus what has actually been explored,
and that being 3,956.23 miles (3,963-6.77).

Should make you wonder, "What is the record
distance mankind has flown over the face of the
Earth?"

The record for the greatest distance a man has
traveled from Earth allegedly occurred April 1970,
when the crew of NASA's Apollo 13 mission swung
around the far side of the moon at an altitude of
158 miles, putting them 248,655 miles (400,171

km) away from Earth. This record has stood now for almost 50 years. [e]

Though, how can we be certain that actually is the record?

This question should be raised in our minds because of conflicting information provided by the NASA organization itself. On March 16, 2015, while Euronews's Claudio Rosmino was performing an interview with two astronauts, Terry W. Virts and Samantha Cristoforettia, who were allegedly aboard the International Space Station (ISS) while it was performing its standard orbital route the following question was asked: [f]

Samantha Cristoforettia (left) and Terry W. Virts (right) performing their typical ISS performance using wires and harnesses.

Claudio (interviewer): "What comes after the international space station, once its mission is over? How do we ensure the continued presence of humans in space?"

Terry Virts (ISS Commander): "Well, that is a great question. The plan that NASA has is to build a rocket called SLS (Space Launch System) which is a heavy-lift rocket, it is something that is much bigger than what we have today and it will be able to launch the Orion capsule with humans on board as well as landers or other components to destinations beyond Earth orbit. *Right now we can only fly in Earth orbit, that is the farthest that we can go. This new system that we are building is going to allow us to go beyond and hopefully take humans into the solar system to explore, so the Moon, Mars, asteroids, there are a lot of destinations that we could go to and we're building these building block components in order to allow us to do that eventually.*"

How could Terry forget that it was in 1969 that NASA's Apollo 11 mission successfully landed on the Moon?

Also, which Earth orbit is Terry referring to?

According to NASA, there are essentially three Earth Orbits: low, mid and high. [g] Low orbit is where the ISS is stationed, that being no greater than 1,242 miles from the surface of Earth, and just beyond that point is the beginning of a dangerous radiation known as the Van Allen Belts. And things get even more confusing when learning about the challenges of the Van Allen Belts radiation from a NASA Engineer.

Kelly Smith, NASA Engineer, who works on Navigation and Guidance for the Orion Capsule expressed that his primary concern is the ability to safely pass through the Van Allen Belts, which consists of dangerous radiation. In fact, he is quoted as saying, "As we get further away from Earth we'll pass through the Van Allen Belts, an area of dangerous radiation. Radiation like this could harm the guidance systems, onboard computers, or other electronics on Orion. Naturally, we have to pass through this danger zone twice. Once up and once back. But Orion has protection. Shielding will be put to the test as the vehicle cuts through the waves of radiation. Sensors aboard will record radiation levels for scientists to study. We must solve these challenges before we send people through this region of space."

Why is it that April 1969 the Van Allen Belts were not a problem for the Moon landing mission, and now it is? How lucky was NASA to be able complete, with no prior test runs, the Moon mission without any issues? Incredible!!! Or is it?

How is it that NASA can send other space crafts (manned/unmanned) that have gone well beyond the Van Allen Belts, including to places like Mars? Those same successful spacecraft technologies, which avoid the dangerous radiation from the Van Allen Belts, still must be re-discovered and re-invented through the Orion Capsule? This is quite confusing.

Can you guess when and who was the first man to circumnavigate the entirety of Antarctica? Your guess is as good as any because you'll not find one shred of documentation that supports the claim since it's never happened. The irony of it is the US had advanced technology to allegedly send men to the Moon, however, they've yet to document the circumnavigation of Antarctica. Do you wonder why that may be? Perhaps, the Moon missions never happened, and Antarctica can't be circumnavigated.

So, what does God's Word say regarding the measurements of His Earth?

According to Jeremiah 31:37 (RSB) it states: "Thus saith Yahweh; If heaven above can be measured, and the foundation of the earth searched out beneath, I will also cast off all the seed of Israel for all that they have done, saith Yahweh."

God is serious about maintaining the secrecy of the dimensions of His Earth. Also, the existence of Israel is yet another proof that all the dimensions of the globular shaped Earth must be a fraud. Of course, assuming you trust God's Word over man's words? If God's Word is faithful and true, would not Israel already be cast off according to Jeremiah 31:37?

Now, let's take a look at Proverbs 25:3 (RSB). It states, "The heaven for height, and the earth for depth, and the heart of kings is unsearchable."

Just as the heart of kings is unsearchable, it is also for the height of heaven and the depth of Earth. And if you accept Yeshua as your Lord and Savior and repent, you can take comfort in the assurance that your sins have been completely forgiven and are separated from you as far as the depths of the sea are unsearchable. Micah 7:19 (RSB) agrees with this concept when it states: "He will turn again, he will have compassion upon us; he will subdue our iniquities; and thou wilt cast all their sins into the depths of the sea."

If you have not accepted Yeshua as your Lord and Savior and repented of your sins, the worst time to consider doing so is after you have died. Once your physical body has died, you are not given an opportunity to accept Yeshua's gift of eternal life. You must choose to live in faith while you are physically alive, as it takes no faith once you see Hell. So, please do this now if you have not yet done so!

Romans 10:9-11 (RSB) says: "That if thou shalt confess with thy mouth the Master Yahshua, and shalt believe in thine heart that Yahweh hath raised him from the dead, thou shalt be saved. For with the heart man believeth unto righteousness; and with the mouth confession is made unto salvation. For the scripture saith, WHOSOEVER BELIEVETH ON HIM SHALL NOT BE ASHAMED."

So, let's recap real quickly.

Worldly Knowledge says: "Through conflicting messages from several sources who work for NASA, the measurements of the Earth, from top to bottom and everywhere in between is already known."

Knowledge, which is just another term for "science," of God says: "The height of heaven and depth of Earth is as unsearchable as the heart of kings, and if these measurements were known then all the seed of Israel would be cast off."

Worldly knowledge is not harmonious with Godly knowledge, even as it pertains to the measurements of the Earth. For you to trust worldly knowledge, it requires abandoning God's Word as being faithful and true, in order, to negotiate even the slightest possibility that worldly knowledge can be mixed with Godly knowledge.

Do you unconditionally believe all of God's Word to be Faithful and True?

BALL VS. CIRCLE

Does it anywhere state in the Bible that the Earth is a ball (aka sphere)?

Interestingly, the shape of the Earth is described in the book of Isaiah, and in the very same book it uses the Hebrew word for "ball" (Strong's Hebrew 1754). However, the Hebrew word "ball" is NOT used to describe the shape of the Earth, instead, the author uses the Hebrew word for "circle" to describe the shape of the Earth. He knew the difference. Please, let me further explain.

In Isaiah 22:18 the author uses the Hebrew word for "ball" (Strong's Hebrew 1754), which can also be used to mean "circle." Isaiah 40:22, uses the Hebrew word for "circle" (Strong's Hebrew 2329) that is sometimes translated as disk, which cannot be used to mean "ball." Isaiah 40:22, is a scripture used to describe the shape of the Earth as distinctly a circle, when if the author was supposed to describe it as a ball could have done so since there is evidence in Isaiah 22:18 that he understood the difference. He described the shape of the Earth as a circle, NOT a ball.

Has Isaiah, the author of the book, accidentally used the wrong word? Was this inspired man of God delusional regarding the shape of the Earth? Or, could it be that the man inspired by God has written what is faithful and true?

Strong's Hebrew Dictionary has assigned lexicon # 1754 to the word ball in Isaiah 22:18. The Hebrew word can be translated to mean "a circle, ball or pile, turn, or round about." Strong's Hebrew Dictionary has assigned lexicon # 2329 to the word circle in Isaiah 40:22. The Hebrew word can also be translated to mean "a circle, circuit, compass."

I believe it beneficial to compare Isaiah 22:18 and Isaiah 40:22 using a few different English translation versions of the Bible.

First, we'll study four different translations for Isaiah 22:18:

The Restoration Study Bible translates Isaiah 22:18 as: "He will surely violently turn and toss thee like a *ball* into a large country: there shalt thou die, and there the chariots of thy glory shall be the shame of thy sovereign's house."

The New International Version translates Isaiah 22:18 as: "He will roll you up tightly like a *ball* and throw you into a large country. There you will die and there the chariots you were so proud of will become a disgrace to   your master's house."

The Amplified Bible translates Isaiah 22:18 as: "And roll you up tightly like a *ball* And toss you into a vast country; There you will die And there your splendid chariots will be, You shame of your master's house."

The International Standard Version translates Isaiah 22:18 as: "rolling you up tightly like a *ball* and throwing you into a large country. There you will die, and there your splendid chariots will lie. You're a disgrace to your master's house!"

Now, let's study four different translations for Isaiah 40:22:

The Restoration Study Bible translates Isaiah 40:22 as: "It is he that sitteth upon the *circle* of the earth, and the inhabitants thereof are as grasshoppers; that stretcheth out the heavens as a curtain, and spreadeth them out as a tent to dwell in:"

The New International Version translates Isaiah 40:22 as: "He sits enthroned above the *circle* of the earth, and its people are like grasshoppers. He stretches out the heavens like a canopy, and spreads them out like a tent to live in."

The Amplified Bible translates Isaiah 40:22 as: "It is He who sits above the *circle* of the earth, And its inhabitants are like grasshoppers; [It is He] who stretches out the heavens like a veil And spreads them out like a tent to   dwell in."

The International Standard Version translates Isaiah 40:22 as: "He's the one who sits above the *disk* of the earth, and its inhabitants are like grasshoppers. He's the one who stretches out the heavens like a curtain, and spreads them like a tent to live in,"

I have seen many times where analogies within the Bible are confused with literalness, and Isaiah 22:18 is no exception. Too many Bible believers have inappropriately dismissed Isaiah 40:22, and other literal descriptions of the Earth, for a cute metaphor or analogy from an ignorant man. Who in this case the "ignorant man" would have to be to Isaiah, the inspired author of God's Word. You might think him to be an "ignorant man," though not me.

Isaiah 22:18 describe rolling up a people group into a tight ball and throwing them into a large country. Many Heliocentrists, who proclaim to be Bible believers, may believe they have grounds for dismissing the fact that Isaiah 40:22 states the shape of the Earth to be a circle (not a ball) because Isaiah 22:18 just sounds too ridiculous to be taken literally. For the man who has made the mistake of agreeing with that mindset, he has utterly missed the phrase "like a ball" in Isaiah 22:18. The word "like" means a "likeness," and not something precisely defined.

And going back to my earlier point, if the metaphor found within Isaiah 22:18 is grounds for dismissing the literalness for a circular/disk shaped Earth (Isaiah 40:22), then where does this illogical philosophy cease? Does it apply to John 3:16, if not, why? Of course, I am being facetious. Though, I use this tone to stress the importance of interpreting scriptures within the eight rules of Hermeneutics.

However, if God wishes to roll up a people group tightly into a ball shape and toss them, then I will not challenge the threat since He can do whatever He pleases. Isaiah 22:18 is meant to be an obvious metaphor, whereas, Isaiah 40:22 is a literal and known fact.

Another verse you may find interesting is Job 38:13-14. Have you ever read it?

The Restoration Study Bible has translated Job 38:13-14 as: "That it might take hold of the ends of the earth, that the wicked might be shaken out of it? It is turned as clay to the seal; and they stand as a garment."

The New International Version has translated Job 38:13-14 as: "that it might take the earth by the edges and shake the wicked out of it? The earth takes shape like clay under a seal; its features stand out like those of a garment."

The Amplified Bible has translated Job 38:13-14 as: "So that light may take hold of the corners of the earth And shake the wickedness out of it? The earth is changed like clay into which a seal is pressed; And the things [of the earth] stand out like a [multi-colored] garment."

The International Standard Version has translated Job 38:13-14 as: "where it seizes the edge of the earth and shakes the wicked out of it? Like clay is molded by a signet ring, the earth's hills and valleys then stand out like the colors of a garment."

What is it supposed to mean that the Earth is shaped like a "seal" or "signet ring" with hills and valleys? While I don't rely too much on Wikipedia for the deeper meanings of life, I believe there are some uses for it. So, let's take a look at what Wikipedia has to say about the historical purposes and characteristics of a "seal" or "signet ring."

*"A seal is a device for making an impression in wax, clay, paper, or some other medium, including an embossment on paper, and is also the impression thus made. The original purpose was to authenticate a document, a wrapper for one such as a modern envelope, or the cover of a container or package holding valuables or other objects....Most seals have always given a single impression on an essentially **flat surface**..." [h]*

Wow! So, according to Job 38:14 the Earth is "like" a flat surface with hills that pop-up out of it and valleys that go down just like a seal/signet ring would be used on wax to seal and authenticate an official document. With the understanding that the Bible is the ultimate authority for truth on this

Earth, and if the Earth was a ball/sphere, then the "likeness" conveyed in Job 38:14 should have agreed with that theory, right? However, it does not. In fact, Job 38:14 is clearly in agreement with Isaiah 40:22 and its account that the Earth is like a flat surface, as a circle (not a ball) would be. Interesting, isn't it?

Do you absolutely believe all of God's Word to be Faithful and True?

STRETCHED LINE

"Where wast thou when I laid the foundations of the earth?...or who hath stretched the line upon it?" - Job 38:4-5 (RSB)

What does it mean to "stretched the line upon it?" Are we really supposed to believe that God is stating that, for the foundations of the Earth to be measured it would require a straight line?

If the Earth is a globe, then it would not be practical and correct to use a straight line to measure it as God's Word demands in Job 38:5. So, why is a straight line required for the Earth's measurement? Maybe, because the Earth is flat?

If the Earth were a globe (aka ball/sphere), would spherical trigonometry (which incorporates the Pythagorean Theorem) not certainly be necessary to measure the Earth? Yes, it would be necessary!

And on a Globe Earth that supposedly has a circumference of 24,901 miles, the drop of the horizon is calculable at approximately 8 inches for every mile squared. Furthermore, the alleged curvature of the Earth is as animated as Mickey Mouse and Daffy Duck through the use of Go-Pro cameras with a Fish-eye lens and Photoshop. Through your God-given senses, your very own eyes tell you that no matter how high your altitude the horizon ALWAYS raises to your eye level.

There are many great calculators on the Internet to help you determine the alleged drop below the horizon to verify the curvature of a globe shaped Earth, and I strongly encourage you to do so. Just be certain you are using the proper calculation. Otherwise, you may find yourself using a calculator that is not the most accurate depiction of drop below the horizon from the eye level of an observer who is standing straight up and looking towards the horizon equally as straight. Some calculators are useful for determining the Earth's bulge, and not the drop below the horizon. They are distinctly two different things (Earth bulge vs. drop below the horizon), for two different purposes.

In short, if the Earth had any measurable curvature the Earth bulge calculation would be helpful to determine how much curvature to expect when building, for example, a bridge over a vast distance over the ocean. Or, if the Earth had any measurable curvature the Earth bulge calculation would be helpful in determining how much curvature must be accounted for when laying railroad track. The only problem is that curvature does not exist on the Earth, and never have the architecture plans for a bridge or railroad track laid on the face of the Earth accounted for the alleged curvature of the Earth. The reason for this is because the Earth is a flat plane!

To measure the drop below the horizon, make sure you use the appropriate calculation for your experiments. Feel free to watch on my YouTube channel, YourCurvelessEarth, the video titled "How to produce an IRREFUTABLE FLAT EARTH Experiment???" During that video, I help explain the difference between the "Earth Bulge Calculation" and the "Earth Drop Below the Horizon Calculation." [i]

In any case, it makes no sense to use a straight line to measure a curved surface, and you can be certain that any architect or mathematician, who is being honest, will attest to it.

Do you unashamedly believe all of God's Word to be Faithful and True?

STRAIGHT PATH

God revealed something to me about one of the more commonly used scriptures in the Christian community, and one I have probably heard almost as often as John 3:16. Perhaps, you too are familiar with it? It is Psalm 27:11, "Teach me your way, O Lord; lead me in a straight path."

Psalm 27:11 is a word picture of a man being taught the Lord's ways which parallels walking a straight path. What a great message, as well as, just another Biblical proof that we are living on a Flat Earth.

If God created Earth to be a globe shape and He wanted to teach us His way on His Earth by following Him on a path, could it truly be straight? Think about it, where does a straight line exist on a sphere shaped object? That's right; it doesn't. If God created Earth to be a globe shape then Psalm 27:11 should have been written as: "Teach me your way, O Lord; lead me in a curved path." We both know that the passage does NOT state this in even the slightest way.

If the Earth is not flat, then how are we expected to be able to comprehend and relate to walking a straight path if nothing of the sort even exists?

Many other verses would have to be thrown out as obsolete and unreliable scriptures because they too teach paths to be straight; in order to maintain a Globe Earth and denounce a Biblically based stationary and Flat Earth. Each of the following verses is from the King James Version.

"And the kine took **the straight way to the way of Bethshemesh**, and went along the highway, lowing as they went, and turned not aside to the right hand or to the left; and the lords of the Philistines went after them unto the border of Bethshemesh." - 1 Samuel 6:12

"Lead me, O Lord, in thy righteousness because of mine enemies; **make thy way straight** before my face." - Psalm 5:8

"The voice of him that crieth in the wilderness, Prepare ye the way of the Lord, **make straight in the desert a highway for our God**." - Isaiah 40:3

"They shall come with weeping, and with supplications will I lead them: I will cause them to **walk by the rivers of waters in a straight way**, wherein they shall not stumble: for I am a father to Israel, and Ephraim is my firstborn." - Jeremiah 31:9

"For this is he that was spoken of by the prophet Esaias, saying, The voice of one crying in the wilderness, Prepare ye the way of the Lord, **make his paths straight**." - Matthew 3:3

"The voice of one crying in the wilderness, Prepare ye the way of the Lord, **make his paths straight**." - Mark 1:3

"As it is written in the book of the words of Esaias the prophet, saying, The voice of one crying in the wilderness, Prepare ye the way of the Lord, **make his paths straight**." - Luke 3:4

"He said, I am the voice of one crying in the wilderness, **Make straight the way of the Lord**, as said the prophet Esaias." - John 1:23

"Therefore loosing from Troas, we came **with a straight course to Samothracia**, and the next day to Neapolis;" - Acts 16:11

"And it came to pass, that after we were gotten from them, and had launched, we came **with a straight course unto Coos**, and the day following unto Rhodes, and from thence unto Patara:" - Acts 21:1

"And **make straight paths** for your feet, lest that which is lame be turned out of the way; but let it rather be healed." - Hebrews 12:13

It is physically impossible to organically achieve straight or level on a spherically shaped object. For instance, if the Earth were globe-shaped a spirit level would only be level relative to its position, and not to the entirety of the globe-shaped Earth.

When building a structure with any significant distance of the Earth, such as a bridge, if a spirit level is used at any point during its construction it will merely give a false positive of the entirety of the structure being level. However, spirit levels have been used for thousands of years and continue to be sold in stores today because they are reliable and consistent products upon a flat and stationary Earth where water always seeks to find its level.

Do you unapologetically believe all of God's Word to be Faithful and True?

Straightened Water

Job 37:10 (RSB) states: "By the breath of El frost is given: and the breadth of the waters is straitened."

Well, if that does not settle it once and for all, I don't know what will? Since the waters are "straitened," meaning the waters are flattened, then oceans, ponds, streams, rivers, and lake waters can't be curving around a globe. So, the Earth can't be a globe shape, and, instead, must be FLAT!

You may be thinking, "Not so fast! Other Bible translations say the water has become frozen."

Ok, you have a very valid point, so let's explore your point deeper. Let's look at Job 37:10 using the

New International Version: "The breath of God produces ice, and the broad waters become frozen."

What happens when water is left un-manipulated? That's right; it always seeks to find its level, otherwise known as flat and straight. And as previously stated, this is why we have been able to rely on spirit levels for thousands of years to produce buildings that are level.

Have you ever seen a pond or a lake that is frozen? Perhaps, you have even skated on one? Do you ever recall noticing a bulge or hump on the top layer of the ice in the center-most part of the pond or lake? If you do, please go back and check again. I am sorry to have to be the one who breaks the news to you, but you recall incorrectly.

In fact, Lake Baikal is located in Russia and is the largest freshwater lake by volume in the world. If the Earth were a globe then when Lake Baikal freezes it should produce a bulge or hump in its center-most part that measures approximately 20 miles high when being viewed from its furthest shoreline. However, there is no bulge or hump to the lake in even the slightest form and is one of the flattest places on Earth when it freezes. [k]

Ice skater on the frozen Lake Baikal located in Russia.

So, is there a contradiction or inaccuracy between the Bible translations where one translation states the "waters is straightened" and another translation states that the "waters become frozen?" Emphatically, "NO!" I submit to you that each translation version is saying the same exact thing, only in a slightly different way. A body of water that is un-manipulated is straight and flat on its top surface, and when that same body of water becomes frozen, it is still straight and flat. In fact, when water is frozen it becomes even straighter and flatter.

When a body of water is frozen, its firmness maintains straightness through and through on the surface. Whereas, during its unfrozen state it is unable to maintain constant straightness on its surface due to winds, currents, and anything else that might produce ripples on the surface of the water. And no matter how many ripples exist on the surface of a body of water, there is no evidence for the alleged curvature for a globe shaped Earth. Test it for yourself, that's what it took for me to solidify the Flat Earth in my mind as reality and truth.

Do you completely believe all of God's Word to be Faithful and True?

STATIONARY & IMMOVABLE

Has it ever occurred to you, that, perhaps, you can't feel the spin of the Earth because...it's...not spinning? Interestingly, each and every experiment that has ever been concocted to attempt to measure and record the motion of the Earth has unanimously proven otherwise, including the Michelson-Morley experiment [j] and Airy's Failure. [l]

Just as interestingly, many verses in the Bible describe the Earth as stable, fixed, and does not move. And science matches God's Word, again. However, there is not even one verse in the Bible that suggests or even hints that the Earth is spinning, has consistent motion, bouncing, or even crawling at a subtle speed. Though I must admit that the Bible does refer to the Earth shaking, only under the circumstances of God's wrath through natural forces, such as, an earthquake. Each of the following three verses is from the King James Version.

"Then **the earth shook and trembled**; the foundations of heaven moved and shook, because he was wroth." - 2 Samuel 22:8

"Therefore I will shake the heavens, and **the earth shall remove out of her place**, in the wrath of the Lord of hosts, and in the day of his fierce anger." - Isaiah 13:13

"And I beheld when he had opened the sixth seal, and, lo, **there was a great earthquake**; and the sun became black as sackcloth of hair, and the moon became as blood; And the stars of heaven fell unto the earth, even as a fig tree casteth her untimely figs, when she is shaken of a mighty wind." - Revelation 6: 12-13

Now, let's get back to the utter and non-motion of the Earth. There are six unambiguous verses in the Bible, which support the complete and utter non-motion of the Earth. While parts of the scriptures below have been made bold for emphasis, the scriptures that are not bold are no less important. It is my personal belief that the text I've made bold is meant to convey the reality that the God of the Bible is the one true God. He is, indeed, Lord of lords and King of kings who is worthy to be worshipped and praised for evermore since His awesome power and might is made manifest throughout His creation and is verifiable with your God-given senses.

And this brings up another important point before we continue. If you believe you can't trust your senses, how can you have enough sense to determine that your senses are unreliable? Is it possible that you may have bought into a lie that has been sold to you over and over beginning from your infancy through the public INDOCTRINATION school system and enterTRAINment industry?

It is crucial that you not discredit your God-given senses. Without these gifts you voluntarily forfeit your God-given sovereignty and are left to prostrate yourself to the temporary and evil earthly authorities, instead of surrendering your heart to God's Word that is faithful and true. When you do not trust God's Word as He speaks to you through it, you leave yourself exposed to the evil one, and he will take advantage of you for not clinging to what is faithful and true. Beware!

One more thing to consider while reading the following six passages is that if one-half of the passage is not entirely reliable and accurate, can you wholeheartedly rely on the other half of it as being faithful and true? So, if the Earth is not stable, not immovable, and not fixed, then are the other words in the passage just as void? I believe they'd have to be. And, at the very least this type of double mindedness (unbelief) affects your subconscious, which is where the subtlest evils most readily and easily enter your mind and soul.

Do you recall the first sin that took place on Earth was in the Garden of Eden and predicated on questioning the faithfulness and truth of God's Word? When will we learn the lesson that God's Words are always faithful and true?

Now, let's begin our review of the six clearest scriptures that state the Earth is not moving. For each of the scriptures, we'll examine them through the lens of 4 different Bible translations to be as thorough as possible.

First, we'll begin with Psalm 93:1:

The Restoration Study Bible translates Psalm 93:1 as: "Yahweh reigneth, he is clothed with majesty; Yahweh is clothed with strength, wherewith he hath girded himself: **the world also is stablished, that it cannot be moved.**"

The New International Version translates Psalm 93:1 as: "The Lord reigns, he is robed in majesty; the Lord is robed in majesty and armed with strength; **indeed, the world is established, firm and secure.**"

The Amplified Bible translates Psalm 93:1 as: "The Lord reigns, He is clothed with majesty and splendor; The Lord has clothed and encircled Himself with strength; **the world is firmly established, it cannot be moved**."

The International Standard Version translates Psalm 93:1 as: "The Lord reigns! He is clothed in majesty; the Lord is clothed, and he is girded with strength. **Indeed, the world is well established, and cannot be shaken**."

The second scripture we'll review is Psalm 96:10:

The Restoration Study Bible translates Psalm 96:10 as: "Say among the heathen that Yahweh reigneth: **the world also shall be established that it shall not be moved**: he shall judge the people righteously."

The New International Version translates Psalm 96:10 as: "The Lord reigns, he is robed in majesty; the Lord is robed in majesty and armed with strength; **indeed, the world is established, firm and secure**."

The Amplified Bible translates Psalm 96:10 as: "Say among the nations, 'The Lord reigns.' **The world is firmly established, it cannot be moved**; he will judge the peoples with equity."

The International Standard Version translates Psalm 96:10 as: "Declare among the nations, 'The

Lord reigns!' **Indeed, he established the world so that it will not falter.** He will judge people fairly."

The third scripture we'll review is Psalm 104:5:

The Restoration Study Bible translates Psalm 104:5 as: "Who laid the foundations of the earth, that it should not be removed for ever."

The New International Version translates Psalm 104:5 as: "He **set the earth on its foundations; it can never be moved.**"

The Amplified Bible translates Psalm 104:5 as: "He **established the earth on its foundations, So that it will not be moved forever and ever.**"

The International Standard Version translates Psalm 104:5 as: "He **established the earth on its foundations, so that it never falters.**"

The fourth scripture we'll review is Psalm 119:89-90:

The Restoration Study Bible translates Psalm 119:89-90 as: "LAMED. For ever, O Yahweh, thy word is settled in heaven. Thy faithfulness is unto all generations: **thou hast established the earth, and it abideth.**"

The New International Version translates Psalm 119:89-90 as: "Your word, Lord, is eternal; it stands firm in the heavens. Your faithfulness continues through all generations; **you established the earth, and it endures**."

The Amplified Bible translates Psalm 119:89-90 as: "Forever, O Lord, Your word is settled in heaven [standing firm and unchangeable]. Your faithfulness continues from generation to generation; **You have established the earth, and it stands [securely]**."

The International Standard Version translates Psalm 119:89-90 as: "Your word is forever, Lord; it is firmly established in heaven. Your faithfulness continues from generation to generation. **You established the earth, and it stands firm**."

The fifth scripture we'll review is Isaiah 45:18:

The Restoration Study Bible translates Isaiah 45:18 as: "For thus saith Yahweh that created the heavens; **Elohim himself that formed the earth and made it; he hath established it**, he created it not in vain, he formed it to be inhabited: I am Yahweh; and there is none else."

The New International Version translates Isaiah 45:18 as: "For this is what the Lord says—**he who created the heavens, he is God; he who fashioned and made the earth**, he founded it; he did not create it to be empty, but formed it to be inhabited—he says: 'I am the Lord, and there is no other.'"

The Amplified Bible translates Isaiah 45:18 as: "For the Lord, who created the heavens (**He is God, who formed the earth and made it; He established it** and did not create it to be a wasteland, but formed it to be inhabited) says this, 'I am the Lord, and there is no one else.'"

The International Standard Version translates Isaiah 45:18 as: "For this is what the Lord says, who created the heavens—**he is God, and the one who formed the earth and made it, and he is the one who established it**; he didn't create it for chaos, but formed it to be inhabited—'I am the Lord and there is no other.'"

The sixth and final scripture related to the utter non-motion of the Earth that we'll review is 1 Chronicles 16:30:

The Restoration Study Bible translates 1 Chronicles 16:30 as: "Fear before him, all the earth: **the world also shall be stable, that it be not moved.**"

The New International Version translates 1 Chronicles 16:30 as: "Tremble before him, all the earth! **The world is firmly established; it cannot be moved.**"

The Amplified Bible translates 1 Chronicles 16:30 as: "Tremble [reverently] before Him, all the earth; **The world is firmly established, it will not be moved.**"

The International Standard Version translates 1 Chronicles 16:30 as: "Tremble in his presence, all the earth! **Surely the inhabited world stands firm—it cannot be moved**."

Think about it, when did you last purchase a retail product? When you looked at your product to open it, what details were invariably written somewhere on it? That's right, the name of the company or individual responsible for making it. That name written on the product is like the signature, or "seal," claiming responsibility and credit for providing their energy, imagination, and/or resources to make that product. Similarly, I believe the six scriptures referring to the Earth as being, immovable, stable, and fixed are God's inherent "seal" on His Earth, just as Job 38:14 indicates.

He is trying to convey to you that as surely as you experience the Earth as immovable, established, and fixed; you can experience Him in your life through the redemptive power of His Son's, Yeshua, death and resurrection to defeat the sting of death on your behalf. He is calling out for you to know that He is your God. He is pleading with you to humble your heart, and worship Him as you have been created to do from the beginning of time. He is Yahweh, the Lord. Amen.

Before knowing the Earth to be a Geocentric Flat Earth model, I always struggled with a particular verse in the Bible. Perhaps, you too are familiar with it.

Psalm 46:10 (RSB) encourages us to "Be still, and know that I am Elohim: I will be exalted among the heathen, I will be exalted in the earth."

I have always understood what it meant to be "still," though I was always perplexed as to how that could even be possible on a spinning globe shaped Earth that whirls through the galaxy. Now, I get it. The Earth is still and at rest, and for me to be still I simply need to, stop moving.

Do you honestly believe all of God's Word to be Faithful and True?

PILLARS
Many Christians have used Job 26:7 in an attempt to support their Globe Earth "theory." Job 26:7 (KJV) states, "He stretcheth out the north over the empty place, and hangeth the earth upon nothing." This verse is often used out of context as a proof for the existence of "gravity." Though, may I ask, "Why would the Earth need something to hang upon when it is already resting on pillars?" Yes, Biblically speaking the Earth rests upon pillars.

Furthermore, have you ever known a ball or sphere to have pillars within it? Yeah, neither have I. With the Earth being a circle/disk that has landmasses that must be perched higher than sea **level**, it's quite practical to have pillars. Just as you would find a beach house located on the shore to have pillars, to perch its lowest floor level higher than sea level to safe guard it from potential flooding during a storm, so is the flat earth you rest upon.

God's Word references the pillars of the Earth 3 times, so let's explore them using a few different Bible translations.

First, we'll review 1 Samuel 2:8 using 4 different Bible translations:

The Restoration Study Bible translates 1 Samuel 2:8 as: "He raiseth up the poor out of the dust, and lifteth up the beggar from the dunghill, to set them among princes, and to make them inherit the throne of glory: **for the pillars of the earth are Yahweh's, and he hath set the world upon them**."

The New International Version translates 1 Samuel 2:8 as: "He raises the poor from the dust and lifts the needy from the ash heap; he seats them with princes and has them inherit a throne of honor. **'For the foundations of the earth are the Lord's; on them he has set the world.'"**

The Amplified Bible translates 1 Samuel 2:8 as: "He raises up the poor from the dust, He lifts up the needy from the ash heap To make them sit with nobles, And inherit a seat of honor and glory; **For the pillars of the earth are the Lord's, And He set the land on them.**"

The International Standard Version translates 1 Samuel 2:8 as: "He raises the poor up from the dust, he lifts up the needy from the trash heap to make them sit with princes and inherit a seat of honor. **Indeed the pillars of the earth belong to the Lord, and he has set the world on them.**"

Next, we'll review Job 9:6 using 4 different Bible translations:

The Restoration Study Bible translates Job 9:6 as: "Which shaketh the earth out of her place, **and the pillars thereof tremble.**"

The New International Version translates Job 9:6 as: "He shakes the earth from its place and **makes its pillars tremble.**"

The Amplified Bible translates Job 9:6 as: "Who shakes the earth out of its place, **And its pillars tremble;**"

The International Standard Version translates Job 9:6 as: "He shakes the earth from its **orbit**, so that its **foundations** shudder."

Before we proceed with the final verse related to the topic of the Earth having pillars, I must give pause to The International Standard Version interpretation of Job 9:6. It is the only version of the 4 I reference for Job 9:6, which states "foundations," instead of "pillars." This is likely due to the fact that they have a heliocentric mindset, and required them to inappropriately assume the liberty to replace the word "place" with "orbit." I can only imagine that the translators for the ISV must not have been able to accept the truth revealed in the book of Job, so they compromised the rules for transliteration. Oh well, moving on.

Lastly, we'll review Psalm 75:3 using four different Bible translations:

The Restoration Study Bible translates Psalm 75:3 as: "The earth and all the inhabitants thereof are dissolved: **I bear up the pillars of it**. Selah."

The New International Version translates Psalm 75:3 as: "When the earth and all its people quake, **it is I who hold its pillars firm**."

The Amplified Bible translates Psalm 75:3 as: "The earth and all the inhabitants of it melt [in tumultuous times]. **It is I who will steady its pillars**. Selah."

The International Standard Version translates Psalm 75:3 as: "While the earth and all its inhabitants melt away, **it is I who keep its pillars firm**."

Because the Bible states the Earth to have pillars, I believe 2 Peter 3:5 makes even more sense.

"For this they willingly are ignorant of, that by the word of God the heavens were of old, and the earth standing out of the water and in the water:" - 2 Peter 3:5 (KJV)

I too was that ignorant man referred to in 2 Peter 3:5 before investigating the doctrine of the shape of the Earth from a comprehensive Biblical perspective.

Do you genuinely believe all of God's Word to be Faithful and True?

FACE

Does the Earth have a face? According to the Bible, it does. Yes, eyes and a nose. Well, not exactly.

The Earth is referred to having a "face" approximately 38 times in the Bible, and 29 of them are derived from Strong's Hebrew dictionary 6440. The following words are used in the definition for Strong's Hebrew dictionary 6440: "forefront(-part), *straight*, upside."

Interestingly, Merriam-Webster defines "face" as the following:

1) any of the *__plane__* surfaces that bound a geometric solid

2) the principal dressed surface (as of a *__disk__*)

Merriam-Webster defines "plane" as the following:

1) a surface in which if any two points are chosen a *__straight line__* joining them lies wholly in that surface

2) a flat or level surface

Aside from the fact that the term "face" has zero application to a globular shaped Earth, let's pretend that it does. If the Earth were a globe, where would the front portion of it be located? For instance, when looking at a baseball, basketball, or soccer ball; which portion of each object is its "face?" The term "face" has no bearing for these objects. However, if you were to apply that same question to the head of a man, it's easy to identify the front portion ("face") of the "somewhat spherically" shaped head of the man where the eyes, nose, and mouth are located.

When you attempt to apply this same logic to a globe shaped Earth, what do you have to use to define the front of it other than landmasses? If it is the landmasses, every globe you have been provided shows each portion of its surface having some land mass, so how can you determine as to which portion of the globe is more defined "as a face" than another? The answer is, "You can't."

Here are the 29 verses in the Bible where you can find the Earth being referenced as having a face. It's a long list; so get comfortable as we study each of them using the King James Version:

"And God said, Behold, I have given you every herb bearing seed, which is upon **the face of all the earth**, and every tree, in the which is the fruit of a tree yielding seed; to you it shall be for meat." - Genesis 1:29

"Behold, thou hast driven me out this day from **the face of the earth**; and from thy face shall I be hid; and I shall be a fugitive and a vagabond in the earth; and it shall come to pass, that every one that findeth me shall slay me." - Genesis 4:14

"And it came to pass, when men began to multiply on **the face of the earth**, and daughters were born unto them," - Genesis 6:1

"And the Lord said, I will destroy man whom I have created from **the face of the earth**; both man, and beast, and the creeping thing, and the fowls of the air; for it repenteth me that I have made them." - Genesis 6:7

"Of fowls also of the air by sevens, the male and the female; to keep seed alive upon ***the face of all the earth***." - Genesis 7:3

"For yet seven days, and I will cause it to rain upon the earth forty days and forty nights; and every living substance that I have made will I destroy from off ***the face of the earth***." - Genesis 7:4

"But the dove found no rest for the sole of her foot, and she returned unto him into the ark, for the waters were on ***the face of the whole earth***: then he put forth his hand, and took her, and pulled her in unto him into the ark." - Genesis 8:9

"So the Lord scattered them abroad from thence upon ***the face of all the earth***: and they left off to build the city." - Genesis 11:8

"Therefore is the name of it called Babel; because the Lord did there confound the language of all the earth: and from thence did the Lord scatter them abroad upon ***the face of all the earth***." - Genesis 11:9

"And the famine was over all ***the face of the earth***: and Joseph opened all the storehouses, and sold unto the Egyptians; and the famine waxed sore in the land of Egypt." - Genesis 41:56

"Wherefore should the Egyptians speak, and say, For mischief did he bring them out, to slay them in the mountains, and to consume them from **the face of the earth**? Turn from thy fierce wrath, and repent of this evil against thy people." - Exodus 32:12

"For wherein shall it be known here that I and thy people have found grace in thy sight? is it not in that thou goest with us? so shall we be separated, I and thy people, from all the people that are upon **the face of the earth**." - Exodus 33:16

"(Now the man Moses was very meek, above all the men which were upon **the face of the earth**.)" - Numbers 12:3

"(For the Lord thy God is a jealous God among you) lest the anger of the Lord thy God be kindled against thee, and destroy thee from off **the face of the earth**." - Deuteronomy 6:15

"For thou art an holy people unto the Lord thy God: the Lord thy God hath chosen thee to be a special people unto himself, above all people that are upon **the face of the earth**." - Deuteronomy 7:6

"But also thou shalt not cut off thy kindness from my house for ever: no, not when the Lord hath cut off the enemies of David every one from **the face of the earth**." - 1 Samuel 20:15

"And this thing became sin unto the house of Jeroboam, even to cut it off, and to destroy it from off *the face of the earth*." - 1 Kings 13:34

"And it is turned round about by his counsels: that they may do whatsoever he commandeth them upon *the face of the world in the earth*." - Job 37:12

"Thou sendest forth thy spirit, they are created: and thou renewest *the face of the earth*." - Psalm 104:30

"And they shall spread them before the sun, and the moon, and all the host of heaven, whom they have loved, and whom they have served, and after whom they have walked, and whom they have sought, and whom they have worshipped: they shall not be gathered, nor be buried; they shall be for dung upon *the face of the earth*." - Jeremiah 8:2

"They shall die of grievous deaths; they shall not be lamented; neither shall they be buried; but they shall be as dung upon *the face of the earth*: and they shall be consumed by the sword, and by famine; and their carcases shall be meat for the fowls of heaven, and for the beasts of the earth." - Jeremiah 16:4

"And all the kings of the north, far and near, one with another, and all the kingdoms of the world, which are upon **the face of the earth**: and the king of Sheshach shall drink after them." - Jeremiah 25:26

"Therefore thus saith the Lord; Behold, I will cast thee from off *the face of the earth*: this year thou shalt die, because thou hast taught rebellion against the Lord." - Jeremiah 28:16

"My sheep wandered through all the mountains, and upon every high hill: yea, my flock was scattered upon all *the face of the earth*, and none did search or seek after them." Ezekiel 34:6

"So that the fishes of the sea, and the fowls of the heaven, and the beasts of the field, and all creeping things that creep upon the earth, and all the men that are upon *the face of the earth*, shall shake at my presence, and the mountains shall be thrown down, and the steep places shall fall, and every wall shall fall to the ground." - Ezekiel 38:20

"And they shall sever out men of continual employment, passing through the land to bury with the passengers those that remain upon *the face of the earth*, to cleanse it: after the end of seven months shall they search." - Ezekiel 39:14

"It is he that buildeth his stories in the heaven, and hath founded his troop in the earth; he that calleth for the waters of the sea, and poureth them out upon **the face of the earth**: The Lord is his name." - Amos 9:6

"Behold, the eyes of the Lord God are upon the sinful kingdom, and I will destroy it from off **the face of the earth**; saving that I will not utterly destroy the house of Jacob, saith the Lord." - Amos 9:8

"Then said he unto me, This is the curse that goeth forth over **the face of the whole earth**: for every one that stealeth shall be cut off as on this side according to it; and every one that sweareth shall be cut off as on that side according to it." - Zechariah 5:3

Interestingly, the Bible also describes the waters as having a "face", and to be "straight", too.

"...And the Spirit of God moved upon **the face of the waters**." - Genesis 1:2b

"And the waters prevailed, and were increased greatly upon the earth; and the ark went upon **the face of the waters**." - Genesis 7:18

Oddly enough, the waters of the deep have a "face" too.

"And the earth was without form, and void; and darkness was upon **the face of the deep**..." - Genesis 1:2a

"The waters are hid as with a stone, and **the face of the deep is frozen**." - Job 38:30

Are you beginning to get the picture that if you choose to continue to believe in anything other than a flat and stationary Earth with all the Biblical information presented to you within this book that you are by default claiming God's Word is neither Faithful nor True?

Do you undoubtedly believe all of God's Word to be Faithful and True?

ENDS

One of the most common questions people have been trained to ask when introduced to Flat Earth is: "Well, if the Earth is FLAT, what happens when you fall off the edge?"

Okay, I'll attempt to humor you for a brief moment. So, when you fall off of the edge of the Earth, you will land in a huge bowl of M&M's and popcorn that has coolers with chilled double-chocolate milk to drink. TVs suspend in mid air playing your favorite movies in the precise order you wish to view them. And Santa Clause sends his flying reindeer to comfort your every need. Now, let's jump back into reality.

If you were required to identify the ends of a baseball, basketball, bowling ball, tennis ball, soccer ball, or golf ball, how would you? Sorry to break it to you, though it's geometrically impossible. So, how could you even begin to describe where the ends of the Earth are located on a globular shaped Earth?

You guessed it! It's just as impossible.

In total, throughout God's Word, the Earth is referred to having an "end" or "ends" 37 times using 7 different Hebrew/Greek words from Strong's Dictionary.

The most commonly used Hebrew word for "end"/"ends" from Strong's Hebrew Dictionary lexicon # 7097 and is used 15 times. Here is the definition for lexicon # 7097, followed by the 15 Bible verses using the King James Version: "after, border, brim, brink, edge, end, (in-)finite, frontier, outmost coast, quarter, shore, (out-)side, X some, ut(-ter-)most (part)."

"The Lord shall bring a nation against thee from far, from **the end of the earth**, as swift as the eagle flieth; a nation whose tongue thou shalt not understand;" - Deuteronomy 28:49

"And the Lord shall scatter thee among all people, from **the one end of the earth even unto the other**; and there thou shalt serve other gods, which neither thou nor thy fathers have known, even wood and stone." -   Deuteronomy 28:64

"He maketh wars to cease unto **the end of the earth**; he breaketh the bow, and cutteth the spear in sunder; he burneth the chariot in the fire." - Psalm 46:9

"From **the end of the earth** will I cry unto thee, when my heart is overwhelmed: lead me to the rock that is higher than I." - Psalm 61:2

"He causeth the vapours to ascend from **the ends of the earth**; he maketh lightnings for the rain; he bringeth the wind out of his treasuries." - Psalm 135:7

"Wisdom is before him that hath understanding; but the eyes of a fool are in **the ends of the earth**." - Proverbs 17:24

"And he will lift up an ensign to the nations from far, and will hiss unto them from **the end of the earth**: and, behold, they shall come with speed swiftly:" - Isaiah 5:26

"Sing unto the Lord a new song, and his praise from **the end of the earth**, ye that go down to the sea, and all that is therein; the isles, and the inhabitants thereof." - Isaiah 42:10

"I will say to the north, Give up; and to the south, Keep not back: bring my sons from far, and my daughters from **the ends of the earth**;" - Isaiah 43:6

"Go ye forth of Babylon, flee ye from the Chaldeans, with a voice of singing declare ye, tell this, utter it **even to the end of the earth**; say ye, The Lord hath redeemed his servant Jacob." - Isaiah 48:20

"And he said, It is a light thing that thou shouldest be my servant to raise up the tribes of Jacob, and to restore the preserved of Israel: I will also give thee for a light to the Gentiles, that thou mayest be my salvation unto *the end of the earth*." - Isaiah 49:6

"When he uttereth his voice, there is a multitude of waters in the heavens, and he causeth the vapours to ascend from *the ends of the earth*; he maketh lightnings with rain, and bringeth forth the wind out of his treasures." - Jeremiah 10:13

"A noise shall come even to *the ends of the earth*; for the Lord hath a controversy with the nations, he will plead with all flesh; he will give them that are wicked to the sword, saith the Lord." - Jeremiah 25:31

"And the slain of the Lord shall be at that day from *one end of the earth even unto the other end of the earth*: they shall not be lamented, neither gathered, nor buried; they shall be dung upon the ground." - Jeremiah 25:33

"When he uttereth his voice, there is a multitude of waters in the heavens; and he causeth the vapours to ascend from **the ends of the earth**: he maketh lightnings with rain, and bringeth forth the wind out of his treasures." - Jeremiah 51:16

The second most commonly used Hebrew word for "end"/"ends" from Strong's Hebrew Dictionary lexicon # 657 and is used 12 times. Here is the definition for lexicon # 657, followed by the 12 Bible verses using the King James Version: "cessation, i.e. an end (especially of the Earth); often used adverb, no further; also (like 'pa`al' (6466)) the ankle (in the dual), as being the extremity of the leg or foot:--ankle, but (only), end, howbeit, less than nothing, nevertheless (where), no, none (beside), not (any, -withstanding), thing of nought, save(-ing), there, uttermost part, want, without (cause)."

"His glory is like the firstling of his bullock, and his horns are like the horns of unicorns: with them he shall push the people together to **the ends of the earth**: and they are the ten thousands of Ephraim, and they are the thousands of Manasseh." - Deuteronomy 33:17

"The adversaries of the Lord shall be broken to pieces; out of heaven shall he thunder upon them: the Lord shall judge **the ends of the earth**; and he shall give strength unto his king, and exalt the horn of his anointed." - 1 Samuel 2:10

"Consume them in wrath, consume them, that they may not be: and let them know that God ruleth in Jacob unto ***the ends of the earth***. Selah." - Psalm 59:13

"God shall bless us; and ***all the ends of the earth*** shall fear him." - Psalm 67:7

"He shall have dominion also from sea to sea, and from the river unto ***the ends of the earth***." - Psalm 72:8

"He hath remembered his mercy and his truth toward the house of Israel: ***all the ends of the earth*** have seen the salvation of our God." - Psalm 98:3

"Who hath ascended up into heaven, or descended? who hath gathered the wind in his fists? who hath bound the waters in a garment? who hath ***established all the ends of the earth***? what is his name, and what is his son's name, if thou canst tell?" - Proverbs 30:4

"Look unto me, and be ye saved, ***all the ends of the earth***: for I am God, and there is none else." - Isaiah 45:22

"The Lord hath made bare his holy arm in the eyes of all the nations; and ***all the ends of the earth*** shall see the salvation of our God." - Isaiah 52:10

"O Lord, my strength, and my fortress, and my refuge in the day of affliction, the Gentiles shall come unto thee from ***the ends of the earth***, and shall say, Surely our fathers have inherited lies, vanity, and things wherein there is no profit." - Jeremiah 16:19

"And he shall stand and feed in the strength of the Lord, in the majesty of the name of the Lord his God; and they shall abide: for now shall he be great unto ***the ends of the earth***." - Micah 5:4

"And I will cut off the chariot from Ephraim, and the horse from Jerusalem, and the battle bow shall be cut off: and he shall speak peace unto the heathen: and his dominion shall be from sea even to sea, and from the river even to ***the ends of the earth***." - Zechariah 9:10

There are two Hebrew words that are tied for third for the use of "end"/"ends", one of them is Strong's Hebrew Dictionary lexicon # 7098 and is used 3 times. Here is the definition for lexicon # 7098, followed by the 3 Bible verses using the King James Version: "a termination (used like 'qatseh' (7097)):--coast, corner, (selv-)edge, lowest, (uttermost) participle".

"Hast thou not known? hast thou not heard, that the everlasting God, the Lord, the Creator of **the ends of the earth**, fainteth not, neither is weary? there is no searching of his understanding." - Isaiah 40:28

"The isles saw it, and feared; **the ends of the earth** were afraid, drew near, and came." - Isaiah 41:5

"Thou whom I have taken from **the ends of the earth**, and called thee from the chief men thereof, and said unto thee, Thou art my servant; I have chosen thee, and not cast thee away." - Isaiah 41:9

The other Hebrew word that is tied for third for the use of "end"/"ends" is Strong's Hebrew Dictionary lexicon # 7099 and is used 3 times. Here is the definition for lexicon # 7099, followed by the 3 Bible verses using the King James Version: "a limit (used like 'qatseh' (7097), but with less variety):-- end, edge, uttermost participle".

"According to thy name, O God, so is thy praise unto **the ends of the earth**: thy right hand is full of righteousness." - Psalm 48:10

"By terrible things in righteousness wilt thou answer us, O God of our salvation; who art the confidence of all **the ends of the earth**, and of them that are afar off upon the sea:" - Psalm 65:5

"Thou hast increased the nation, O Lord, thou hast increased the nation: thou art glorified: thou hadst removed it far unto **all the ends of the earth**." - Isaiah 26:15

The fourth most commonly used Hebrew word for "end"/"ends" from Strong's Hebrew Dictionary is lexicon # 3671 and is used twice. Here is the definition for lexicon # 3671, followed by the 2 Bible verses using the King James Version: "an edge or extremity; specifically (of a bird or army) a wing, (of a garment or bed-clothing) a flap, (of the earth) a quarter, (of a building) a pinnacle:--+ bird, border, corner, end, feather(-ed), X flying, + (one an-)other, overspreading, X quarters, skirt, X sort, uttermost part, wing((-ed))."

"He directeth it under the whole heaven, and his lightning unto **the ends of the earth**." - Job 37:3

"That it might take hold of **the ends of the earth**, that the wicked might be shaken out of it?" - Job 38:13

Two words are tied for fifth for the use of "end"/"ends", and one of them is from Strong's Hebrew Dictionary lexicon # 5491 and is used only once. Here is the definition for lexicon # 5491, followed by the Bible verse using the King James Version: "--end."

"It is thou, O king, that art grown and become strong: for thy greatness is grown, and reacheth unto heaven, and thy dominion to **the end of the earth**." - Daniel 4:22

The other word tied for fifth for the use of "end"/"ends" is from Strong's Greek Dictionary 5491 and is used only once. Here is the definition for 5491, followed by the Bible verse that uses it: "farthest, final (of place or time):--ends of, last, latter end, lowest, uttermost."

"For so hath the Lord commanded us, saying, I have set thee to be a light of the Gentiles, that thou shouldest be for salvation unto **the ends of the earth**." - Acts 13:47

Again, I must ask you to think, why are all these inspired authors of God's Word using words to describe the shape of the Earth as having a border, having an edge, coming to a cessation, not being able to go any further, having an uttermost part, having geometric terminations, being the farthest, and being the final/last part? Especially, if it doesn't matter what the shape is, why is the shape of the Earth mentioned so often? Perhaps, it does matter? Maybe not to most, but it must have mattered enough to God that it is spoken about a lot. And, none of the words they use can be associated to a globular, ball, sphere, or oblate spheroid shaped Earth.

You have a choice to make regarding God's Word, and that is one of the two options:

1. It is NOT Faithful, and it is NOT True, or

2. It is Faithful, and it is True.

You may be thinking, "Why don't you just go to Antarctica and see if there is an end/edge of the Earth, and if you don't fall off then you are right?" I would love to, however, there only remains one huge obstacle in my path, and for all other independent explorers for that matter. It's called the Antarctic Treaty and was initially signed by 12 countries in 1959, and is now comprised of 59 countries.[j] No one is permitted to perform truly free and independent explorations of Antarctica. If you don't believe me, just take 15 – 30 minutes to research Jarle Andehoy. If any explorations occur in Antarctica, it is extremely monitored and controlled.

But, what are "they" hiding? When you've time, I strongly encourage you to research Admiral Richard E. Byrd who spent extensive time, without restriction, exploring the North Pole and Antarctica during the 1940s and 1950s. To give you a glimpse at what he experienced, I have transcribed a portion of one of his last publically syndicated television interviews. Go onto YouTube to watch it in full. [m]

Admiral Richard E. Byrd, a Freemason.

Admiral Richard E. Byrd was asked the following during a publicly recorded interview on a television program named Longines Chronoscope: *"Well Admiral Byrd, I think everyone can understand why the interest in the North Pole, because its so near our greatest challenger, Soviet Russia. But, why this interest in the bottom of the world? Nobody living down there, is there?"*

Admiral Richard E. Byrd replied: *"I'll tell you one reason they are interested. It's by far the most, uh, valuable and important place in the world for science. That's where the scientific groups all over the nation really are interested. But more important than that, it has to do with the future of the nation. For those to come after us, or even during your lifetime. Because it happens to be an untouched reservoir of natural resources."*

Later in the interview he was asked the following question: *"Admiral, you speak of the resources of Antarctica, what are they? What, uh, what are the natural resources there?"*

Admiral Richard E. Byrd replied: *"Well, eh, we've found enough coal within 180 miles of the South Pole in a great, ah, ridge of mountains. It's not covered with snow. Enough to supply the whole world for quite a while. Ah, that's...that's the coal. Now, there's evidence of many other minerals. We're pretty sure there's oil. Now, that coal shows the bottom of the world now by far the coldest spot in the world where that coal is it gets 100 below zero in the winter. There it once was tropical. So, uh, we think there's oil and evidence probably of uranium there."*

Then Admiral Byrd was asked: *"Well, Admiral Byrd, are private expeditions a thing of the past? Is expedition and exploration now purely a government function because of the tremendous cost to an organization?"*

Admiral Byrd replied: *"Ah, no, I don't think so. I think down south it may be more less a thing of a past. But not other...other expeditions. A lot of them going off now."*

Interviewer asked: *"Admiral Byrd, may I ask you, is there a great difference in the top of the world from the bottom of the world?"*

Admiral Byrd replied: *"Ah, there is. Now, the North Pole is the center of an ocean 10,000 feet deep. The South Pole is the center of a plateau 10,000 feet high. The North Pole, ya see, is surrounded by continents slightly frozen. The Antarctic continent is surrounded by a belt of ice, frozen seas, and is at least 12,000 miles thick. Now, the south is a plateau that gets in some places 14,000 feet up. Ah, I've been in areas over 13,000, and it's a little bit chilly up there. So, there's that big difference between the top and bottom of the world. The north really isn't that cold up there on the arctic ocean."*

So, why is the public deterred and prohibited from independent exploration of Antarctica? Per Admiral Byrd, it's because of the abundant natural resources. Additionally, according to Admiral Richard E. Byrd, no one is able to fall off of the end/edge of the Earth because there's an ice wall that extends as high as 14,000 feet above the face of the ocean. You just may be interested in researching Operation Highjump, which took place between 1946 and 1947.

Not surprisingly man's observations of the Earth validate God's Word as Faithful and True.

According to Proverbs 8:29 (KJV), "When he gave to the sea his decree, that the waters should not pass his commandment: when he appointed the foundations of the earth:"

Do you truly believe all of God's Word to be Faithful and True?

CORNERS

Have you ever seen a spherically shaped sports ball, like basketball or soccer ball, with a corner? Maybe a flat ball can have a corner, though definitely NOT an inflated one.

There are two mentions in God's Word for the Earth having literal corners, and four distinct corners to be more precise.

First, we'll review Isaiah 11:12 using four different Bible translations:

The Restoration Study Bible translates Isaiah 11:12 as: "And he shall set up an ensign for the nations, and shall assemble the outcasts of Israel, and gather together the dispersed of Judah **from the four corners of the earth**."

The New International Version translates Isaiah 11:12 as: "He will raise a banner for the nations and gather the exiles of Israel; he will assemble the scattered people of Judah **from the four quarters of the earth**."

The Amplified Bible translates Isaiah 11:12 as: "And He will lift up a signal for the nations And assemble the outcasts of Israel, And will gather the dispersed of Judah **From the four corners of the earth**."

The International Standard Version translates Isaiah 11:12 as: "He will raise a banner for the nations and will assemble the dispersed of Israel; he will gather the scattered people of Judah **from the corners of the earth**."

Now, we'll review Revelation 7:1 using four different Bible translations:

The Restoration Study Bible translates Revelation 7:1 as: "And after these things I **saw four angels standing on the four corners of the earth**, holding the four winds of the earth, that the wind should not blow on the earth, nor on the sea, nor on any tree."

The New International Version translates Revelation 7:1 as: "After this I **saw four angels standing at the four corners of the earth**, holding back the four winds of the earth to prevent any wind from blowing on the land or on the sea or on any tree."

The Amplified Bible translates Revelation 7:1 as: "After this I **saw four angels stationed at the four corners of the earth**, holding back the four winds of the earth so that no wind would blow on the earth or on the sea or on any tree."

The International Standard Version translates Revelation 7:1 as: "After this, I **saw four angels standing at the four corners of the earth**. They were holding back the four winds of the earth so that no wind could blow on the land, on the sea, or on any tree."

Whether these four corners of the Earth are reachable within the firmament, a topic to be covered later on, or are just outside of the firmament I probably won't know until I die and go to heaven. At which point, I could care less. However, while situated in my finite body on this Earth, it is intriguing and would love the opportunity to explore it for myself. Of course, just as soon as I can figure a way to explore the Antarctic independently!

Do you trust that the authors of the Bible are truly inspired by God? Do you trust the inspired authors written account of the geometrical shape of God's Earth? If not, why? Is it just too much to believe that the "authorities" of this world have again been caught in a lie?

Do you wholeheartedly believe all of God's Word to be Faithful and True?

FIRMAMENT (AKA DOME)

The word "firmament" is used 16 times in 15 different Bible verses. And, here's a pop quiz for you. How many firmaments are mentioned in the Bible? Is it 3? Is it 4? Maybe, 2? Nope.

There is only one firmament mentioned in God's Word and appropriately its mentioned for the first time in the Biblical account of Creation.

"And Elohim said, Let there be **a firmament** in the midst of the waters, and let it divide the waters from the waters. And Elohim made **the firmament**, and divided the waters which were under **the**

firmament from the waters which were above **the firmament**: and it was so. And Elohim called **the firmament** Heaven. And the evening and the morning were the second day." - Genesis 1:6-8 (RSB)

The reason I mention that there is one and only one firmament is I have witnessed too many professional "Bible Scholars" who have an alphabet soup suffix title (MDV, MABL, etc.) who botch this simple concept. I can only surmise they ruin it so badly to maintain their delusion that the Bible is not definitively describing a flat and stationary Earth. They must have to talk themselves, and, unfortunately, their audience too, into believing that there could be many firmaments to justify the many supposed outer space dimensions or atmospheres above the Globe Earth. Can we please just get back to the basics of interpreting God's Word the way it was intended, in context?

Since we have established the fact that there is only one firmament, now we can explore the deeper questions surrounding it.

WHAT IS THE FIRMAMENT?

The Hebrew word for firmament is raqiya`. Strong's Hebrew Dictionary has assigned lexicon # 7549, and is defined as follows: "properly, an expanse, i.e. the firmament or (apparently) visible arch of the sky:--firmament."

The root Hebrew word for raqiya` is raqa` (enunciated as: raw-kah'), Strong's Hebrew Dictionary 7554, and is defined as follows: "to pound the earth (as a sign of passion); by analogy to expand (by hammering); by implication, to overlay (with thin sheets of metal):--beat, make broad, spread abroad (forth, over, out, into plates), stamp, stretch."

Based on the definitions of these words, the best we can make is that the firmament is a solid and firm substance that has been beat out and stretched over the face of the Earth and is the expanse above your head in the visible arch of the sky. Many English Bible translations use the word "dome," instead of, firmament.

Merriam-Webster dictionary defines dome as: "a large hemispherical roof or ceiling."

Isaiah 40:22 from the Restoration Study Bible states that God "...stretcheth out the heavens as a curtain, and spreadeth them out as a tent to dwell in." When Isaiah said tent, he knew what a tent looks like and so do you. In short, it's a covering that goes from the ground and raised overhead that creates a space between the covering overhead and the surface beneath one's feet.

How do you figure a tent structure is supposed to fit properly over a ball/sphere? It doesn't.

WHERE IS THE FIRMAMENT?
According to God's Word, it is over your head...right now. Take a look outside.

How high is it? How far does it extend from one end of the Earth to the other end of the Earth? Not sure, and if you recall from the chapter named "Measurements," we actually are not supposed to know. The following two verses are from the Restoration Study Bible.

"Thus saith Yahweh; If heaven above can be measured, and the foundation of the earth searched out beneath, I will also cast off all the seed of Israel for all that they have done, saith Yahweh." - Jeremiah 31:37

"The heaven for height, and the earth for depth, and the heart of kings is unsearchable." - Proverbs 25:3

Another noteworthy subject related to the height of the dome is Operation Fishbowl. It took place between April and November of 1962, and may just be something you would be interested in further investigating.

WHY DOES THE FIRMAMENT EXIST?

According to the Word of God, that is Faithful and True, the firmament has a spiritual application and practical application.

Spiritually speaking, the firmament has been overhead since the beginning of Creation as a testament to God's handiwork and power who is worthy to be praised forevermore. Each of the following verses are from the Restoration Study Bible, unless otherwise stated.

"The heavens declare the glory of El; and the firmament sheweth his handywork." - Psalm 19:1

"Praise ye Yah. Praise El in his sanctuary: praise him in the firmament of his power." - Psalm 150: 1

Practically speaking, the firmament does many things. Firstly, it divides the waters.

"And Elohim said, Let there be a firmament in the midst of the waters, and let it divide the waters from the waters. And Elohim made the firmament, and divided the waters which were under the firmament from the waters which were above the firmament: and it was so." - Genesis 1:6-7

So, not only is water beneath our feet, there is water above our heads on just the other side of the firmament. In fact, with the latest camera zoom technology, like a Nikon P900, zoom in on a star on a clear night sky, and you will likely be able to see what appears to be ripples of water that glistens over what seems to be like an electrical orb, called a star.

For the firmament to divide the waters under the firmament from the waters above the firmament, the firmament must be solid. And, what do you know, there just so happens to be a verse that exists which supports that realistic assumption.

Job 37:18 from the King James Version Bible states: "Hast thou with him spread out the sky, which is strong, and as a molten looking glass?"

Secondly, the firmament has served as a floodgate for the waters above and the waters below. The firmament was used to help flood the entire Earth.

"In the six hundredth year of Noah's life, in the second month, the seventeenth day of the month, the same day were all the fountains of the great deep broken up, and the windows of heaven were opened." - Genesis 7:11

When the Lord was finished flooding the entire Earth during the days of Noah, the firmament was used to restrain the water.

According to Genesis 8:2 from the King James Version, "The fountains also of the deep and the windows of heaven were stopped, and the rain from heaven was restrained;"

Thirdly, the firmament is where the natural lights are located, including, the stars for signs, and for seasons, and for days, and years.

"And Elohim said, Let there be lights in the firmament of the heaven to divide the day from the night; and let them be for signs, and for seasons, and for days, and years: And let them be for lights in the firmament of the heaven to give light upon the earth: and it was so. And Elohim made two great lights; the greater light to rule the day, and the lesser light to rule the night: he made the stars also. And Elohim set them in the firmament of the heaven to give light upon the earth, And to rule over the day and over the night, and to divide the light from the darkness: and Elohim saw that it was good." - Genesis 1:14-18

Please, take note that God never makes mention of creating "planets" in His Word. Some translations replace the commonly translated word "constellations" with "planets." For example, the Restoration Study Bible for 2 Kings 23:5. However, nowhere is it stated that God created a "planet."

All images of "planets," according to NASA's website, are merely CGI (computer-generated imagery). When analyzing some of the older images from NASA they appear to be paintings by "Photo Realist" artists, nothing more and nothing less.

Fourthly, the firmament is for open space allowing the creatures that walk the face of the Earth to move about, including, the ability for the fowl to fly above the face of the Earth in the open firmament of heaven.

"And Elohim said, Let the waters bring forth abundantly the moving creature that hath life, and fowl that may fly above the earth in the open firmament of heaven." – Genesis 1:20

Spiritually and practically speaking, the throne of God is over the firmament and the Earth serving as God's footstool.

"Thus saith Yahweh, The heaven is my throne, and the earth is my footstool: where is the house that ye build unto me? and where is the place of my rest?" - Isaiah 66:1

"Then I looked, and, behold, in the firmament that was above the head of the cherubims there appeared over them as it were a sapphire stone, as the appearance of the likeness of a throne." - Ezekiel 10:1

"But I say unto you, Swear not at all; neither by heaven; for it is Yahweh's throne: Nor by the earth; for it is his footstool: neither by Jerusalem; for it is the city of the great King." - Matthew 5:34-35 (RSB)

"And he that shall swear by heaven, sweareth by the throne of Yahweh, and by him that sitteth thereon." - Matthew 23:22

"But will Elohim indeed dwell on the earth? behold, the heaven and heaven of heavens cannot contain thee; how much less this house that I have builded?" - 1 Kings 8:27

Additionally, the literal firmament can be used for analogies, and wouldn't be possible if the firmament from its onset was supposed to be interpreted as solely a poetic imagery, figurative expression, or a loose analogy.

"And the likeness of the firmament upon the heads of the living creature was as the colour of the terrible crystal, stretched forth over their heads above. And under the firmament were their wings straight, the one toward the other: every one had two, which covered on this side, and every one had two, which covered on that side, their bodies. And when they went, I heard the noise of their wings, like the noise of great waters, as the voice of the Almighty, the voice of speech, as the noise of an host: when they stood, they let down their wings. And there was a voice from the firmament that was over their heads, when they stood, and had let down their wings. And above the firmament that was over their heads was the likeness of a throne, as the appearance of a sapphire stone: and upon the likeness of the throne was the likeness as the appearance of a man above upon it." - Ezekiel 1:22-26

"And they that be wise shall shine as the brightness of the firmament; and they that turn many to righteousness as the stars for ever and ever." - Daniel 12:3

Regarding the firmament, you may find it extremely interesting that Wernher von Braun, famous NASA employee who was world renowned for rocket development between the 1930s and 1970s put one verse on his tombstone. Psalm 19:1 is inscribed on his tombstone.

"The heavens declare the glory of El; and the firmament sheweth his handywork." - Psalm 19:1

Was he trying to tell you something that he wasn't permitted to say publically?

If you'd like to see the tombstone for yourself, it is located at Ivy Hill Cemetery, 2823 King Street, Alexandria, Virginia [22302]. And, if you want to see an image that excellently depicts a Biblically based Earth and firmament, I highly recommend you researching keyword "Rob Skiba Terrarium."

Do you firmly believe all of God's Word to be Faithful and True?

SUN

Have you ever considered that, perhaps, the Sun is moving over your head while the Earth beneath your feet is not moving? Well, that's also what the inspired authors of God's Word knew to be true, so they wrote it that way. In fact, when looking at all the verses that describe the motion of the Sun it is described as such: arise, raiseth, arose, down, go down, goeth down, going down, gone down, moved, backward, no more go down, rise, risen, riseth, riseth not, rising, rose, sunrising, up, went down.

If the Sun isn't supposed to be moving relative to the position of the Earth (per the heliocentric Globe Earth model), then each of the following 55 scriptures from the King James Version listed below from God's Word is neither faithful nor true.

"And when ***the sun was going down***, a deep sleep fell upon Abram; and, lo, an horror of great darkness fell upon him." - Genesis 15:12

"And it came to pass, that, when ***the sun went down***, and it was dark, behold a smoking furnace, and a burning lamp that passed between those pieces." - Genesis 15:17

"***The sun was risen upon the earth*** when Lot entered into Zoar." - Genesis 19:23

"And as he passed over Penuel ***the sun rose*** upon him, and he halted upon his thigh." - Genesis 32:31

"But Moses hands were heavy; and they took a stone, and put it under him, and he sat thereon; and Aaron and Hur stayed up his hands, the one on the one side, and the other on the other side; and his hands were steady until ***the going down of the sun***." - Exodus 17:12

"If ***the sun be risen*** upon him, there shall be blood shed for him; for he should make full restitution; if he have nothing, then he shall be sold for his theft." - Exodus 22:3

"If thou at all take thy neighbour's raiment to pledge, thou shalt deliver it unto him by that ***the sun goeth down***:" - Exodus 22:26

"And when **the sun is down**, he shall be clean, and shall afterward eat of the holy things; because it is his food." - Leviticus 22:7

"And on the east side toward **the rising of the sun** shall they of the standard of the camp of Judah pitch throughout their armies: and Nahshon the son of Amminadab shall be captain of the children of Judah." - Numbers 2:3

"And they journeyed from Oboth, and pitched at Ijeabarim, in the wilderness which is before Moab, toward **the sunrising**." - Numbers 21:11

"The two tribes and the half tribe have received their inheritance on this side Jordan near Jericho eastward, toward **the sunrising**." - Numbers 34:15

"Then Moses severed three cities on this side Jordan toward **the sunrising**;" - Deuteronomy 4:41

"And they possessed his land, and the land of Og king of Bashan, two kings of the Amorites, which were on this side Jordan toward **the sunrising**;" - Deuteronomy 4:47

"Are they not on the other side Jordan, by the way where **the sun goeth down**, in the land of the Canaanites, which dwell in the champaign over against Gilgal, beside the plains of Moreh?" - Deuteronomy 11:30

"But at the place which the Lord thy God shall choose to place his name in, there thou shalt sacrifice the passover at even, at **the going down of the sun**, at the season that thou camest forth out of Egypt." - Deuteronomy 16:6

"But it shall be, when evening cometh on, he shall wash himself with water: and when **the sun is down**, he shall come into the camp again." - Deuteronomy 23:11

"In any case thou shalt deliver him the pledge again when **the sun goeth down**, that he may sleep in his own raiment, and bless thee: and it shall be righteousness unto thee before the Lord thy God." - Deuteronomy 24:13

"At his day thou shalt give him his hire, neither shall **the sun go down** upon it; for he is poor, and setteth his heart upon it: lest he cry against thee unto the Lord, and it be sin unto thee." - Deuteronomy 24:15

"until the Lord gives them rest, as he has done for you, and until they too have taken possession of the land the Lord your God is giving them. After that, you may go back and occupy your own land, which Moses the servant of the Lord gave you east of the Jordan toward **the sunrise**." - Joshua 1:15

"And the king of Ai he hanged on a tree until eventide: and as soon as **the sun was down**, Joshua commanded that they should take his carcase down from the tree, and cast it at the entering of the gate of the city, and raise thereon a great heap of stones, that remaineth unto this day." - Joshua 8:29

"And it came to pass at the time of **the going down of the sun**, that Joshua commanded, and they took them down off the trees, and cast them into the cave wherein they had been hid, and laid great stones in the cave's mouth, which remain until this very day." - Joshua 10:27

"Now these are the kings of the land, which the children of Israel smote, and possessed their land on the other side Jordan toward **the rising of the sun**, from the river Arnon unto mount Hermon, and all the plain on the east:" - Joshua 12:1

"And the land of the Giblites, and all Lebanon, toward **the sunrising**, from Baalgad under mount Hermon unto the entering into Hamath." - Joshua 13:5

"And turned from Sarid eastward toward **the sunrising** unto the border of Chislothtabor, and then goeth out to Daberath, and goeth up to Japhia," - Joshua 19:12

"And turneth toward **the sunrising** to Bethdagon, and reacheth to Zebulun, and to the valley of Jiphthahel toward the north side of Bethemek, and

Neiel, and goeth out to Cabul on the left hand," - Joshua 19:27

"And then the coast turneth westward to Aznothtabor, and goeth out from thence to Hukkok, and reacheth to Zebulun on the south side, and reacheth to Asher on the west side, and to Judah upon Jordan toward *the sunrising*." - Joshua 19:34

"And Gideon the son of Joash returned from battle before *the sun was up*," - Judges 8:13

"And it shall be, that in the morning, as soon as *the sun is up*, thou shalt rise early, and set upon the city: and, behold, when he and the people that is with him come out against thee, then mayest thou do to them as thou shalt find occasion." - Judges 9:33

"And the men of the city said unto him on the seventh day before *the sun went down*, What is sweeter than honey? And what is stronger than a lion? and he said unto them, If ye had not plowed with my heifer, ye had not found out my riddle." - Judges 14:18

"And they passed on and went their way; and *the sun went down* upon them when they were by Gibeah, which belongeth to Benjamin." - Judges 19:14

"Thus they inclosed the Benjamites round about, and chased them, and trode them down with ease over against Gibeah toward **the sunrising**." - Judges 20:43

"Joab also and Abishai pursued after Abner: and **the sun went down** when they were come to the hill of Ammah, that lieth before Giah by the way of the wilderness of Gibeon." - 2 Samuel 2:24

"And when all the people came to cause David to eat meat while it was yet day, David sware, saying, So do God to me, and more also, if I taste bread, or ought else, till **the sun be down**." - 2 Samuel 3:35

"And he shall be as the light of the morning, **when the sun riseth**, even a morning without clouds; as the tender grass springing out of the earth by clear shining after rain." - 2 Samuel 23:4

"And there went a proclamation throughout the host about **the going down of the sun**, saying, Every man to his city, and every man to his own country." - 1 Kings 22:36

"And the battle increased that day: howbeit the king of Israel stayed himself up in his chariot against the Syrians until the even: and about **the time of the sun going down** he died." - 2 Chronicles 18:34

"The mighty God, even the Lord, hath spoken, and called the earth from **the rising of the sun unto the going down thereof**." - Psalm 50:1

"From **the rising of the sun unto the going down of the same** the Lord's name is to be praised." - Psalm 113:3

"The sun also ariseth, and the sun goeth down, and hasteth to his place where he arose." - Ecclesiastes 1:5

"I have raised up one from the north, and he shall come: from **the rising of the sun** shall he call upon my name: and he shall come upon princes as upon morter, and as the potter treadeth clay." - Isaiah 41:25

"That they may know from **the rising of the sun**, and from the west, that there is none beside me. I am the Lord, and there is none else." - Isaiah 45:6

"So shall they fear the name of the Lord from the west, and his glory from **the rising of the sun**. When the enemy shall come in like a flood, the Spirit of the Lord shall lift up a standard against him." - Isaiah 59:19

"'The mother of seven will grow faint and breathe her last. Her **sun will set** while it is still day; she will be disgraced and humiliated. I will put the survivors to the sword before their enemies,' declares the Lord." - Jeremiah 15:9

"Then the king, when he heard these words, was sore displeased with himself, and set his heart on Daniel to deliver him: and he laboured till ***the going down of the sun*** to deliver him." - Daniel 6:14

"And it shall come to pass in that day, saith the Lord God, that I will cause ***the sun to go down*** at noon, and I will darken the earth in the clear day:" - Amos 8:9

"When the ***sun rose***, God provided a scorching east wind, and the sun blazed on Jonah's head so that he grew faint. He wanted to die, and said, 'It would be better for me to die than to live.'" - Jonah 4:8

"Therefore night shall be unto you, that ye shall not have a vision; and it shall be dark unto you, that ye shall not divine; and ***the sun shall go down*** over the prophets, and the day shall be dark over them." - Micah 3:6

"Thy crowned are as the locusts, and thy captains as the great grasshoppers, which camp in the hedges in the cold day, but when ***the sun ariseth*** they flee away, and their place is not known where they are." - Nahum 3:17

"For from **the rising of the sun even unto the going down of the same** my name shall be great among the Gentiles; and in every place incense shall be offered unto my name, and a pure offering: for my name shall be great among the heathen, saith the Lord of hosts." - Malachi 1:11

"That ye may be the children of your Father which is in heaven: **for he maketh his sun to rise** on the evil and on the good, and sendeth rain on the just and on the unjust." - Matthew 5:45

"And very early in the morning the first day of the week, they came unto the sepulchre at **the rising of the sun**." - Mark 16:2

"Be ye angry, and sin not: let not **the sun go down** upon your wrath:" - Ephesians 4:26

"For **the sun is no sooner risen** with a burning heat, but it withereth the grass, and the flower thereof falleth, and the grace of the fashion of it perisheth: so also shall the rich man fade away in his ways." - James 1:11

Interestingly, God's Word supports the non-motion of the Sun in only four particular instances. Each of the following verses are from the Restoration Study Bible:

"Thy **sun shall no more go down**; neither shall thy moon withdraw itself: for Yahweh shall be thine everlasting light, and the days of thy mourning shall be ended." - Isaiah 60:20

"Which **commandeth the sun, and it riseth not**; and sealeth up the stars." - Job 9:7

"Then spake Joshua to Yahweh in the day when Yahweh delivered up the Amorites before the children of Israel, and he said in the sight of Israel, **Sun, stand thou still** upon Gibeon; and thou, Moon, in the valley of Ajalon. And **the sun stood still**, and the moon stayed, until the people had avenged themselves upon their enemies. Is not this written in the book of Jasher? So **the sun stood still in the midst of heaven, and hasted not to go down about a whole day.** And there was no day like that before it or after it, that Yahweh hearkened unto the voice of a man: for Yahweh fought for Israel." - Joshua 10:12-14

"**The sun *and* moon stood still in their habitation**: at the light of thine arrows they went, *and* at the shining of thy glittering spear." - Habakkuk 3:11

Now, let's think about this for a minute. For sake of argument, let's suppose the Earth is a globe-shaped object that orbits the Sun while it's rotating on its axis. And, this being the reason the Sun merely appears to be moving relative to the Earth though is not, then why is it that four different inspired authors of God's Word wrote about the non-motion of the Sun as being truly an uncommon occurrence:

1) "sun shall no more go down" (Isaiah 60:20)

2) "commandeth the sun, and it riseth not" (Job 9:7)

3) "Sun, stand still" (Joshua 10:12)

4) "sun stood still" (stated twice in Joshua 10:13)

5) "sun and moon stood still in their habitation" (Habakkuk 3:11)

If the Sun was already "not moving," then why is it that Isaiah 60:20 states that the "...sun shall no more go down" and Job 9:7 says, "commandeth the sun, and it riseth not?" For the Sun to stop moving would imply that it first had to be moving from its onset. If the Earth is a spinning globe, should not the authors have said that the Earth shall no more orbit the Sun and the Earth shall spin no more? It certainly should have if the Earth is a globe spinning on its axis and orbiting the Sun, though God's Word does not state that at all. Why is this? Well, because according to God's Word, that is Faithful and True, the Earth is stationary and flat with the Sun orbiting overhead on a circuit, that's why.

Also, why is it that Joshua 10:13 states that the "sun stood still?" If the Earth were a spinning globe that orbits the Sun, then the Sun would already be still and motionless relative to the Earth, and his command to make the Sun stand still would be wasted and illogical words.

Perhaps, the Sun is NOT stationary relative to the Earth? Perhaps, the Sun is actually traveling on a circuit above the stationary and Flat Earth, and when the Sun stood still it was an anomaly? If you believe God's Word to be Faithful and True, what other explanation have you?

And if you are interested in understanding how the seasons work on the Flat Earth, among many other related topics, on the stationary and Flat Earth, I highly recommend you read "Zetetic Astronomy: Earth Not a Globe" written by Samuel Birley Rowbotham.

Do you unquestionably believe all of God's Word to be Faithful and True?

MOON

How much time do you believe you have you spent analyzing the patterns of the Moon? Has it been long enough to realize that the Moon is not rotating on its axis? You've been taught from the very beginning of your education that the Moon spins on its axis while it orbits the Globe Earth. You can observe and verify with your own eyes if this is what you see.

When you observe the Moon with any consistency, do not be surprised to realize that the same portion of the Moon is always facing you no matter the vantage point you see it on the face of the Earth during its cycle. Additionally, it rotates in a clockwise motion while it circuits overhead displaying its same portion, like a wheel.

So, if the Earth is stationary and flat with the Sun circuiting overhead, is the Moon's light still solely the reflection of the sunlight?

Nope. Not at least according to God's Word, which is Faithful and True. Accordingly, the Moon has its own light, which is not reflecting from the Sun. There are nine verses that state the Moon has its own light, and two of the scriptures are literally from Jesus's mouth by the account of the inspired author of God's Word. Each of the following verses are from the Restoration Study Bible.

"And Elohim made two great lights; the greater light [sun] to rule the day, and **the lesser light [moon] to rule the night**: he made the stars also." - Genesis 1:16

"For the stars of heaven and the constellations thereof shall not give their light: the sun shall be darkened in his going forth, and **the moon shall not cause her light to shine**." - Isaiah 13:10

The following verse states that the moon shall be *as* the light of the moon, not that it will be the light or reflection of the sun.

"Moreover **the light of the moon shall be <u>as</u> the light of the sun**, and the light of the sun shall be sevenfold, as the light of seven days, in the day that Yahweh bindeth up the breach of his people, and healeth the stroke of their wound." - Isaiah 30:26

"The sun shall be no more thy light by day; **neither for brightness shall the moon give light unto thee**: but Yahweh shall be unto thee an everlasting light, and thy Elohim thy glory." - Isaiah 60:19-20

"Thus saith Yahweh, which giveth the sun for a light by day, and the ordinances of **the moon and of the**

stars for a light by night, which divideth the sea when the waves thereof roar; Yahweh of hosts is his name:" - Jeremiah 31:35

"Immediately after the tribulation of those days shall the sun be darkened, and **the moon shall not give her light**, and the stars shall fall from heaven, and the powers of the heavens shall be shaken:" - Matthew 24:29

"But in those days, after that tribulation, the sun shall be darkened, and **the moon shall not give her light**," - Mark 13:24

"And when I shall put thee out, I will cover the heaven, and make the stars thereof dark; I will cover the sun with a cloud, **and the moon shall not give her light**." - Ezekiel 32:7

"And **the city had no need of** the sun, neither of **the moon, to shine in it**: for the glory of Elohim did lighten it, and the Lamb is the light thereof." - Revelation 21:23

When I, and many others, have independently tested the temperature of the Moonlight on the ground, and then on the same night tested the temperature beneath the shade (not in the Moonlight) the temperature is higher under the shade than in the direct Moonlight, which is a lower temperature. If the light of the Moon were a reflection of the Sun, then its heat would respond similarly. Thereby, in direct Moonlight, the temperature should be greater than in the shadow. However, you will find just the opposite result. Test and see for yourself.

Per God's Word, He is not like man that he should lie.

"...let Elohim be true, but every man a liar..." - Romans 3:4

"El is not a man, that he should lie; neither the son of man, that he should repent: hath he said, and shall he not do it? or hath he spoken, and shall he not make it good?" - Numbers 23:19

"Who hath ascended up into heaven, or descended? who hath gathered the wind in his fists? who hath bound the waters in a garment? who hath established all the ends of the earth? what is his name, and what is his son's name, if thou canst tell? Every word of Eloah is pure: he is a shield unto them that put their trust in him. Add thou not unto his words, lest he reprove thee, and thou be found a liar." - Proverbs 30:4-6

I must admit that some of the deeper spiritually things of life I've been able to more readily accept as I've embraced wholeheartedly that God's Word is Faithful and True. This is what Jesus said to the Pharisee named Nicodemus: "If I have told you earthly things, and ye believe not, how shall ye believe, if I tell you of heavenly things?" – John 3:12

And Jesus's words are just as applicable and relevant today as they were then. Amen!

This too includes the "dominion" God gave man. Genesis 1:26 from the King James Version says, "And God said, Let us make man in our image, after our likeness: and let them have dominion over the fish of the sea, and over the fowl of the air, and over the cattle, and over all the earth, and over every creeping thing that creepeth upon the earth."

Notice, God gave man dominion over the fish of the sea, the fowl of the air, over the cattle all over the Earth, and over every creeping thing that creepeth upon the Earth. So, how does that tie into the topic of the Moon? Well, think about it for just a moment. Did God give man dominion over the Moon? Well, not according to His word. Which should prompt you with the following inquiry, "How is it that man was able to land on the Moon and have dominion on it when God did NOT give him dominion over it?" And, rhetorically you should by now be able to answer yourself with a resounding, "Man has never been to the Moon."

Do you undeniably believe all of God's Word to be Faithful and True?

HIGH ALTITUDE PERSPECTIVES

What is the highest altitude you have been? If you have flown on a plane, you have likely been at an altitude between 35,000 feet and 40,000 feet. When converted to miles, that is between 6.62 miles and 7.57 miles. And, something to quickly note is that the thing you fly on is called a "plane" because it flies over a "plane," also known as the Flat Earth.

Now, if you fly during the daytime, you will observe the horizon as always remaining at eye level, and no curvature is detectable from your right to your left as far as your eyes can see. And if you believe you see curvature through the curved shaped window from the plane, it is nothing more than a distortion caused by the curvature in your oval-shaped window. Just the same as you experience through a camera with a fish-eye lens.

If the Earth were a globe-shaped object, it would be physically impossible given what we know about our natural world for the horizon to ALWAYS raise to eye level and remain FLAT. In fact, the higher the altitude one goes up the observer should be required to look further down to keep the horizon at eye level, and should notice curvature to the right and to the left. This is never the case.

In fact, 3 scriptures match precisely to the reality you, and I experience.

The first two verses are found in Daniel chapter 4 and are an account of a vision king Nebuchadnezzar had. In his vision, he saw a tree with a height that reached so high up into the heaven that an observer looking from the top of the tree could view the ends of the Earth.

You may be thinking, "But this is just a vision. So, what's the big deal?"

Well, first of all, we have already been able to ascertain from the chapter titled "Ends" that ends do NOT exist on a globe-shaped object. And even though his vision is only a vision it is already in alignment with all other scripture accounts of the shape of the Earth, and that being flat.

Secondly, on a globe-shaped Earth, it is a physical impossibility, without at least some amazingly huge and perfectly angled mirrors, to view every side of a spherically shaped object from only one perspective or vantage point. However, on a Flat Earth, it's practical and easy to comprehend.

Here are the two verses from the King James Version regarding the extremely tall tree Nebuchadnezzar references within his vision.

"The tree grew, and was strong, and the height thereof reached unto heaven, and **the sight thereof to the end of all the earth**:" - Daniel 4:11

"The tree that thou sawest, which grew, and was strong, **whose height reached unto the heaven, and the sight thereof to all the earth**;" - Daniel 4:20

Then there is that time when the devil tempted Jesus. During this account, the devil takes Jesus up to a high mountain, and then shows him all the kingdoms of the world. How can this even be possible to see all the kingdoms of the world on a globe-shaped Earth? It's not. Is it possible on a Flat Earth? Well, with the mountain being high and if the skies were clear, what else is required with the Earth being FLAT? The following passage is from the King James Version:

"Again, the devil **taketh him up into an exceeding high mountain, and sheweth him all the kingdoms of the world**, and the glory of them;" - Matthew 4:8

Do you sincerely believe all of God's Word to be Faithful and True?

EVERYONE SEES JESUS
"Behold, he cometh with clouds; and *every eye shall see him*, and they also which pierced him: and all kindreds of the earth shall wail because of him. Even so, Amen." - Revelation 1:7 (RSB)

How is it possible that every eye will see Jesus if we are living on a physically shaped ball? That is physically impossible. Many have speculated that every eye shall see Jesus return using their television, computer, smartphone device, and tablet device. And from an unbiblical Heliocentric Universe model, I'd understand why someone would have to imagine Jesus's second coming from that perspective.

However, I'd like to propose another perspective. A Biblical one, if I may. Since the Earth is stationary and flat from a Biblical perspective, what if Jesus is quite large, perhaps, bigger than the Sun and Moon? And, what if He will be high up in the sky, greater than the altitude of the Sun and the Moon? If all this were true, then it would be possible from any location on Earth for an observer to use his eye and see Jesus. In fact, if they were to use a device to see Him, it would not be their eye that sees Him. Instead, it would be the transmission of another device that sees him and that image being projected on a digital device. Thus, their eyes are on a digital device and NOT on Jesus.

Do you fervently believe all of God's Word to be Faithful and True?

NEW JERUSALEM

After Yeshua, who is Faithful and True, has made His second coming then a New Jerusalem will be established. Yes, VERY exciting times for those who are being saved by the blood of Jesus Christ.

Though, there's something a bit peculiar about this New Jerusalem that we should contemplate when considering the doctrine of the shape of the Earth. And, if you are at all familiar with Bible Prophecy, then you may even know what direction I am headed with this topic. That's right, the dimensions of the New Jerusalem make-up a HUGE shaped cube. Let's take a look at the passage, and then we'll dive deeper.

"And he that talked with me had a golden reed to measure the city, and the gates thereof, and the wall thereof. And the city lieth foursquare, and the length is as large as the breadth: and he measured the city with the reed, twelve thousand furlongs. The length and the breadth and the height of it are equal. And he measured the wall thereof, an hundred and forty and four cubits, according to the measure of a man, that is, of the angel." - Revelation 21:15-17 (KJV)

While these units of measure may seem foreign to us, they were well known at the time the book of Revelation was written. And, as Revelation 21:17 states, they are "the measure of a man." In other words, the measurements given are measures understood by man.

The exact dimensions of New Jerusalem were measured by an angel and reported to be 12,000 furlongs or stadia, which is the equivalent of 1,500 miles or 2,414 kilometers, in length, width, and height. If New Jerusalem were located in the middle of the United States, it would stretch from Canada to Mexico and from the Appalachian Mountains to the border of California.

What's even more astounding is the height of New Jerusalem will be 1,500 miles. To put this into perspective, let's consider the altitude of the Sun upon the face of the Flat Earth. Much of the research floating around in the Flat Earth forums suggest the Sun to be somewhere between 300 miles and 3,000 miles above the face of the Earth. If the Sun is only 300 miles high, then the height of New Jerusalem will be 5 times higher than the Sun. And at that proportion, New Jerusalem would likely be visible to an observer from any location upon the Flat Earth. Even if the Sun were 3,000 miles above the face of the Earth, the height of the New Jerusalem would be halfway to the altitude of the Sun and be visible for an observer from many locations on the Flat Earth.

If you recall, according to the Globe Earth model, there is an 8-inch per mile-squared drop below the horizon. According to the Globe Earth model, straight lines and attaining true level is geometrically impossible. So, how is the New Jerusalem, which is a huge cube-shaped object, supposed to practically fit upon a globular shaped Earth? Perhaps, the standard "Scientific" answer would be, "A LOT of gravity."

Or maybe, the answer is a Biblically based stationary and Flat Earth? Why do we have to make things so difficult on ourselves by justifying lies and dismissing the truth, when the answers have been in God's Word this entire time? Lord, please forgive us!

Do you passionately believe all of God's Word to be Faithful and True?

CHAPTER 4: WHERE DOES THE BIBLE SAY "FLAT EARTH"?

If the Bible points to a Flat Earth with each one of its descriptions about the Earth, why doesn't at least one verse in the Bible just say the words "Flat Earth?" Well, it does. It just depends on which Bible you read.

Have you ever heard of the William Tyndale Bible or the Matthews Bible? In 1530, the William Tyndale Bible became the very first English translation of a Bible. The Matthews Bible followed shortly thereafter-in 1537. While I have heard claims that the William Tyndale Bible and the Matthews Bible translations both use the term "flat earth" in 2 Samuel 11:11, I have only been able to confirm for the Matthews Bible. And as for the King James Version Bible, and all other translations after it, the term "flat earth" has been replaced with "open fields."

The Matthews Bible 1537 translates 2 Samuel 11:11 as follows: "And Urias said unto David: the ark and Israel and Juda dwell in pavilions: and my lord Joab and the servants of my lord lie in tents upon the **flat earth**: and should I then go into mine house, to eat and to drink and to lie with my wife? By thy life and as sure as thy soul liveth I will not do that thing."[n]

The King James Version Bible translates 2 Samuel 11:11 as follows: "And Uriah said unto David, The ark, and Israel, and Judah, abide in tents; and my lord Joab, and the servants of my lord, are encamped in the **open fields**; shall I then go into mine house, to eat and to drink, and to lie with my wife? as thou livest, and as thy soul liveth, I will not do this thing."

If you are a "King James Version ONLY" proponent, this comparison of scriptures should at the very least cause some pause for you to at least consider whether or not a King James Version ONLY Bible is truly the ONLY Bible worthy of your Biblical study.

Now, when someone asks you, "Where does the Bible say the words 'Flat Earth?'" you are soundly equipped with a knowledgeable response.

CHAPTER 5: CREATION WORSHIPPERS

Because this topic is quite uncomfortable to discuss, I would prefer to ignore it completely. And, since I can't, then I will do the next best thing and make it as brief as possible.

So, who is responsible for the Satanically based Globe Earth heresy? You guessed it, Satan worshippers who are also known as Creation Worshippers in God's Word. These folks have been around since just about the beginning of time and well documented within God's Word. They are the continuation of Babylonian pagan Sun-god worship.

Today, these people still exist and hide in secret societies. While most of the participants of the organizations are a lower rank and remain ignorant to the worship of Satan by their higher-ranking members, they are unknowingly working directly for an organization that pushes Satan's agenda, a "New World Order."

A few of the more prominent organizations include the Freemasons, Shriners, and Jesuits. There is so much information publically available on this particular topic a citation is not necessary to back up these statements. It's known in the public domain, just take an hour or two and research it.

People within these organizations themselves have believed a lie that they can live in duality, and be the enforcers of both good and evil. One of their common phrases is "As below so above," which means to "Bring hell on Earth." And not surprisingly, they are not regarded highly in God's eyes, as you will see in a few of the following verses from the Restoration Study Bible, unless notated otherwise.

"And lest thou lift up thine eyes unto heaven, and when thou seest the sun, and the moon, and the stars, even all the host of heaven, shouldest be driven to worship them, and serve them..." - Deuteronomy 4:19

"If there be found among you, within any of thy gates which Yahweh thy Elohim giveth thee, man or woman, that hath wrought wickedness in the sight of Yahweh thy Elohim, in transgressing his covenant, And hath gone and served other mighty ones, and worshipped them, either the sun, or moon, or any of the host of heaven, which I have not commanded; And it be told thee, and thou hast heard of it, and enquired diligently, and, behold, it be true, and the thing certain, that such abomination is wrought in Israel: Then shalt thou bring forth that man or that woman, which have committed that wicked thing, unto thy gates, even that man or that woman, and shalt stone them with stones, till they die." - Deuteronomy 17:3

"He did away with the idolatrous priests appointed by the kings of Judah to burn incense on the high places of the towns of Judah and on those around Jerusalem—those who burned incense to Baal, to the sun and moon, to the constellations and to all the starry hosts." - 2 Kings 23:5 (NIV)

"At that time, saith Yahweh, they shall bring out the bones of the kings of Judah, and the bones of his princes, and the bones of the priests, and the bones of the prophets, and the bones of the inhabitants of Jerusalem, out of their graves: And they shall spread them before the sun, and the moon, and all the host of heaven, whom they have loved, and whom they have served, and after whom they have walked, and whom they have sought, and whom they have worshipped: they shall not be gathered, nor be buried; they shall be for dung upon the face of the earth." - Jeremiah 8:2

If you are in a "secret society" that gives praise or worship to anyone or anything other than Jesus Christ, I pray you come out of that demonic trap and repent and turn to Christ for forgiveness. He loves you!

CHAPTER 6: HOLLOW EARTH NON-SENSE

The Hollow Earth concept has roots in Freemasonry and The Church of Jesus Christ of Latter-day Saints (aka Mormons). The Mormons beliefs at the core denounce the proper deity of Yeshua, and the Freemasons are deeply involved in satanic worship (the worship of Lucifer; the "Light Bearer").[p]

In short, the Hollow Earth concept maintains the Earth to be a Globe Earth; however, at the core of the Globe Earth, it is allegedly hollow, which is where heaven also exists. To enter and exit the Hollow Earth (aka Heaven) one only needs to travel through underground tunnels, the North Pole, or the South Pole.

The foundational premise of the Hollow Theory first requires a Globe Earth, though, is just as delusional as the Globe Earth that is NOT hollow. The non-hollow Globe Earth fantasy provides exploration and adventure. Fantasies like distant planets and stars, whereas, the Hollow Earth is fixated on the endless possibilities that the Earth may contain: advanced races, aliens, spaceships and spaceship bases, 10 Lost Tribes of Israel, Political Kingdom of God, Lost Viking Colonies of Greenland, and an inner Sun that is Heaven.

Hollow Earth does not exist without a Globe Earth. The Bible does NOT support a globe-shaped Earth, thus, the Hollow Earth is just as hollow.

CHAPTER 7: SOLAR ECLIPSE (AUG 21, 2017)

The topic of an eclipse has probably been one of the most common stumbling blocks for those new to the concept of a flat and stationary Earth. On Monday, August 21st, 2017 observers on American soil, beginning in Oregon and ending in South Carolina, were able to observe a Total Solar Eclipse. When in the path of totality of the eclipse it lasted for about 2 minutes and 35 seconds.

I was able to take a few pictures of the Total Solar Eclipse from my driveway in Georgia, and it was an amazing and memorable experience.

If this doctrine is new to you and you are seriously considering the Earth may, in fact, be stationary and flat, then you likely have some big outstanding questions in your mind. For instance, how is it that observers in Oregon were the first to be able to view the solar eclipse? And, how is it that observers in South Carolina were last to be able to see the solar eclipse?

One thing to keep in mind is that everything on the Flat Earth Universe model is much easier than on the Globe Earth Universe model.

Before being able to explain why observers in Oregon saw the solar eclipse first, and then observers in South Carolina saw it last, we must first establish a common, stationary, and level ground. The Sun and Moon are similar, if not exactly the same size.

On Monday, August 21st, 2017 the Sun and the Moon were, as usual. Each on similar circuits moving from east to west, and while both were south of the observer the Sun was more south than the Moon and at a higher altitude upon the face of the Earth.

On their respective circuits, the Sun travels at a faster speed than the Moon. And, on this very day the Sun lapped, or passed, the Moon with the shadow of the Moon cast upon the observer who stood between the direct sunlight of the Sun and the Moon, which obstructed the view of the sunlight and cast a shadow. The observer witnessed the western side of the Sun being eclipsed by the eastward side of the Moon as the Sun began to pass the Moon until the Sun's eastward side had fully moved out of the western side of the Moon.

As a result, observers in Oregon saw the solar eclipse's path of totality at approximately 10:16 am Pacific Time Zone on Monday, August 21st, 2017.

A little later in the day, observers in Kansas saw the solar eclipse's path of totality at approximately 1:05 pm Central Time Zone on Monday, August 21st, 2017.

And, finally, observers in South Carolina saw the solar eclipse's path of totality at approximately 2:47 pm Eastern Time Zone on Monday, August 21st, 2017.

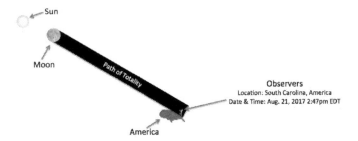

What about the other solar eclipses? Like the one scheduled for April 8, 2024, where an explanation of the Moon getting between the observer and the Sun do NOT match to the approximate circuit of the Moon and Sun?

Well, the best I can say is that I've seen videos of prior solar eclipses filmed from an airplane, and there is evidence of other "hosts," or "orbs," that are not the Moon, near the Sun that can cause a solar eclipse. However, until I see it for myself, I am not quite certain. Furthermore, I'd rather admit that I know what I am not sure of than to blindly believe a lie, which never ceases to espouse such absurd and baseless claims and is definitively contrary to God's Word. Yes, I am referring to that satanic Heliocentric Universe model.

CHAPTER 8: TRUTH LEADS TO YESHUA

For the edification of the body of Christ, the people who are in Yeshua, and have traversed the shape of the Earth discussions and realized there is no other Earth described in the Bible except for a stationary and Flat Earth, we are accountable to share this truth in love. I believe each one of us has a unique testimony, which is the very same way He loves each of us, uniquely. And, while a belief in the shape of the Earth is NOT one's salvation in any way shape or form, it does represent one's level of faith and trust in God's Word.

Lord willing, in a subsequent book, I plan to curate many impactful Flat Earth related testimonies from people all over the face of the Earth. If you are interested in being a part of this project, I will later share with you how you can join. If you do wish to participate there is only one question you need to answer: "As a believer and follower of Jesus Christ, how has the revelation of a Biblically based stationary and Flat Earth impacted my faith in God's Word?"

Here are two real-life testimonies that I hope bless and encourage you as you also consider sharing yours.

DON SCHMOLL

I met Don Schmoll through a Facebook Closed Group called Biblical Flat Earthers. On February 16, 2017, at 8:15 pm Eastern Standard Time he posted the following testimony:

"Why I Believe (100% sure without a doubt) the Earth is Flat?

For me, it all started back in May of 2015. I was at work listening to a live Broadcast of Hagman and Hagman. They were getting towards the end of the broadcast and were taking calls. Somebody came online and started this whole sheeple about us being lied to by the governments of the world and he came right out of nowhere and said the Earth is flat. I immediately started to chuckle, not believing what I had just heard. I think I said, "you gotta be kidding", under my breath. There was silence for a few seconds and the two hosts were kind enough to the caller and basically let him go and the call ended. After that the whole subject was dropped. I was like, okay, wow. Somebody actually believes that? I let it go and forgot about it.

I would like to interject at this point that for the few previous years I have been having my doubts about the heliocentric model and was looking into geocentricity but with the globe. A Flat Earth didn't even cross my mind at that time.

Back to my Flat Earth testimony. I would say it was maybe a week or two after the Hagman and Hagman program, I can't remember, I was mowing my lawn and decided to listen to a podcast hosted by Zen Garcia. His subject was Geocentricity. He started his opening statement and declared that he had come to the conclusion that the Earth is flat. My response was, "Oh, Zen, not you". Up until that time I had great respect for his research. I turned off the podcast and found something else to listen to. I wasn't buying it.

Two weeks later I was sitting at my desk and decided to listen again to what Zen had to say on that program. It was a half hour in and I was having a hard time following him. It was Saturday night so I decided to go to thedgeam.com website to see what Daniel Ott had going on. Well, lo and behold. What was his guest talking about? His guest was none other than Mark Sargent talking about the Flat Earth. Me, being full of the Holy Ghost, told GOD, "OK, you now have my attention." I watch all of the videos Mark Sargent had created. Though I don't agree with everything he says, that was basically a primer.

I began my own personal research and deep seeking in the spirit. I thought to myself, if this is true the Bible has got to reflect it. I found an essay online called The Flat Earth Bible. It was written by an atheist whose purpose was to discredit the Bible. The author is now deceased, but I thanked him for his research anyway. He did a very good job. It's at this website if anyone is interested but be aware he was out to discredit the Bible: https://www.lhup.edu/~dsimanek/febible.htm.

At that point I began my own deep studies in scripture and found that in order for scripture to be true the Earth has to be an enclosed motionless plane. I know that using the Bible argument falls on deaf ears when it comes to those who don't believe the Bible or believe in God. It falls on deaf ears with many who claim that the Bible is inspired writ.

Then I began looking at the sky, the sun, the moon and stars at night. I located Polaris, the North Star, and pondered its position in the sky. The revelation hit me that there is no way that it can be where it is claimed to be, well it is but not over a ball. I have a renewed interest in constantly looking up.

I then opened the Book of Enoch, of which I have three hard copies. I have had it for sometime but could never grasp some of what is in it. But after getting the revelation of the Earth being flat the Book of Enoch just started unfolding itself. Many things began to occur to me. First, there is no doubt that the first Book of Enoch is inspired. The section, "The Courses of the Heavenly Luminaries" tells you much of what you need to know about our true reality. There is absolutely no doubt that the Earth is not a globe in motion, but is a stationary plane. And last but not least, this thing is going viral and there is no stopping it. The Lord began to reveal to me who He wanted me to share this with. Most of whom I shared this with have received it while others are still resisting.

It did not take me going out and doing laser tests or sending up a balloon or any experiments like that...I just know without a doubt. I trust what my senses are telling me. We are not on a spinning ball. We live on a plane. It is a created realm. We are here for a reason and we are important to the one who created this place and us.

People will accuse me of naivety and being gullible because of my lack of experimentation. I have seen enough empirical evidence performed by others with greater means than I have. I would say that naivety and gullibleness is happening in public education where I swallowed the ball Earth heliocentric lie.

For thousands of years man knew that the Earth is an enclosed motionless plane. It took five hundred years for the elites to convince the entire world that the Earth is a spinning globe orbiting a giant sun. It took the multi-billion dollar special effects agency we know as NASA to seal the deal.

I think that the so-called Bible believing holdouts are the most vicious in their attacks because it is not only hitting them where they live but also it is hitting them concerning their holy book. So what do they do? They deny that it's there. Not only that I have seen a lot of this, 2 Timothy 4:3 "For the time will come when they will not endure sound doctrine; but after their own lusts shall they heap to themselves teachers, having itching ears;"

2 Timothy 4:4, "And they shall turn away their ears from the truth, and shall be turned unto fables."

Flat Earth Bible believers are being accused of having itching ears and being turned unto fables. Now wait a minute! This scripture was written roughly two thousand years ago. We're talking fifteen hundred years between the New Testament and the adoption of the heliocentric model by the Catholic Church and Church of England. Both were apostatized churches by that time. Both were turned away from the truth of the Bible and went after the heliocentric fable.

All of our lives we have been living in a time of very great deception. The deception kicked into high gear when NASA was created to bolster the lie. Our God has allowed the truth to come out for a time such as this and there is no stopping it. I thank God that I have been open to the truth and I desire more truth.

We Flat Earthers are coming out of the great deception, the strong delusion. The strong delusion isn't coming, it has been with us for five hundred years. I have become very concerned for those who flat out reject the truth that our Father has revealed to us. The truth coming out is His doing and those who will receive it are receiving it whether they are Christian or not. Praise be to God that many non-believers are coming to Christ after receiving this Flat Earth truth. So if anybody tries to tell you this has nothing to do with salvation shut them down immediately! Praise God! We are living in a great time!"

MELISSA CHANDLEY

I met Melissa Chandley through a Facebook Closed Group called Biblical Flat Earthers. On February 16, 2017, at 9:49 pm Eastern Standard Time she posted the following testimony:

Public POST: "My husband has been [an] atheist ever since I've known him. Just over a month ago, after many years of praying, I believe God has led him to becoming a believer because of Flat Earth!"

While these testimonies are unique, significant, and extremely encouraging, they have the same message. The God of the Bible is the one true God, which has been made plain for us to witness that our physical reality that matches perfectly with God's Word. Both our observation of nature and

God's Word reveal a stationary and Flat Earth, and we serve Him and only Him.

If you feel compelled to testify with me and other fellow Bible Believers that the Earth is stationary and flat because God's Word is always Faithful and True, please email me at nathan@FlatEarthDoctrine.com.

CHAPTER 9: AWAKEN THE SLEEPING CHURCH

If you believe God's Word always to be Faithful and True, then I am pleading with you to please share this book with as many people as you can. In particular, share this book with as many pastors as possible. This message of God's Word is "Faithful and True" needs to be preached from the pulpit to more quickly spread the message to true Yeshua followers who rely on Biblically-based doctrine.

If you still believe the shape of the Earth to be an inconsequential doctrine and are unwilling to adhere and abide in God's Word on the matter, why is that? I mean, what is the hang-up if it doesn't truly matter to you one way or another? Perhaps, it does matter to you, and you are minimalizing the doctrine to justify your refusal to submit to God's Word on the matter.

For example, one of my close friends told me that the shape of the Earth is a complete waste of time and an inconsequential topic. So, I decided to give him an opportunity to prove his point. I encouraged him to just create and publish a post on his social media that stated, "The Earth is Flat." Not surprisingly, he refused. If he believed the shape of the Earth to be a truly inconsequential matter, then he would have had no issue with posting that statement on his social media account. His refusal to oblige my request revealed that the topic of the shape of the Earth is NOT so inconsequential after all. I only hope he too saw, or at least one day may see, the inconsistency in his words and deeds.

However, if you believe God's Word to be Faithful and True, you should not be ashamed of any of it. Even to say to a friend or family member or post on your social media account something to the effect of: "I believe the Earth is Stationary and Flat because God's Word is ALWAYS Faithful and True!" And, if you are a pastor of a church, you should be able to unashamedly preach a sermon on this topic. I am not challenging you to teach on this doctrine because it is your mandate to convince others to believe the Earth to be stationary and flat. However, it is your mandate to teach God's Word in context and to inspire your congregation to live faithful and truthful lives. By testifying that you believe the Earth to be stationary and flat because the "Bible Tells You So," you are testifying that you believe God's Word is ALWAYS "Faithful and True."

I believe it is quite hypocritical for a man who claims to believe the Bible to be the infallible, holy, and inspired Words of God to encourage others to adopt his very same beliefs, while he refuses to submit to even the most basic of Bible doctrines.

The doctrine of the shape of the Earth is a fundamental foundation of a Biblically based faith. It should be embarrassing to church leaders all over the face of the Earth that I, a layman, am a messenger to the church body through this book when the leaders of the church are the ones responsible for knowing sound Biblical doctrines and teaching it to their congregation.

The ignorance that has spread in the church like cancer for hundreds of years regarding the doctrine of the shape of the Earth is evidence enough to me that church leaders have clung more dearly to the thoughts and words of other men who teach about the Bible than adhering directly to God's Word. This astronomically sized mishap in the church should give all of us pause and ask ourselves, "What else do we believe we know about God's Word that is flat out wrong? What have we adopted from the world that we thought to be Godly, and is not?" We need to humble and submit ourselves fully to God's Word, and not to man's words.

I praise God that He is using me in this manner, to edify and build up His church to a stronger maturity. His Word that is always Faithful and True. Amen.

Each time I hear a Pastor, Evangelist, or prominent leader in the "Mainstream Christian" community who says the word "planet" or "globe," I cringe. With that one little word he truly believes he's just declared a widely known and obvious fact of our existence to help add credibility to his sermon or message to connect with an equally delusional audience. I can only imagine, God may be cringing just as much, if not more. We live on a "plane," not a "planet." I pray the word "planet," "globe," and the likes thereof never be spoken again from the mouth of a Bible Believer unless used in the context of exposing the lies of "Worldly Science" through the doctrine of the shape of the Earth from a truly Biblical perspective.

Now, it is time to bring full circuit the heart behind this book that I stated in the "Introduction." Do you recall the heart behind this book? There were two groups of people I seek to encourage in this book, and one of the groups of people are Christians.

I stated the following in regards to the Christian, "Only then will the prayers of believers in Yeshua (Hebrew word for "Jesus") HaMashiac (Hebrew word for "the Messiah") become more relevant, frequent and fervent, and as a result, more powerful and effective." Whether you realize it or not, the prayers of some Christian congregations are petitioned on behalf of demonic forces without their knowledge and consent. Yes, I just said that, and please let me explain.

I have a friend who used to attend the same church in Texas as a NASA Astronaut named Dr. Kjell Norwood Lindgren. Kjell was about to leave for his 2015 International Space Station (ISS) tour, and just before he left he offered my friend an opportunity of a lifetime. If my friend would give him a family photo, then he would take that family photo on his mission to outer space in the ISS and use a camera on the ISS to take a picture of him holding my friend's family photo and send the ISS photo back to my friend. And, just before Kjell's 2015 ISS mission, the entire church congregation in Texas laid hands on him and his family, and then they prayed that Kjell would have a successful and safe space exploration mission. If it were ever possible to pray an irrelevant prayer, that church congregation in Texas was duped into praying it. It's time for real Christians to wake up, because the church has fallen fast asleep.

Though, just because a church wastes a few prayers on an ActorNOT and his fake space mission it doesn't mean they are missing the mark entirely when it comes to serving the one true God, Yahweh. Healthy churches do exist despite being soundly asleep in regards to the doctrine of the shape of the Earth.

How do I know this? Well, I attend and serve at one! The church is filled with great people, and the church leaders obviously desire to serve the Lord and lead His people to do the same. I believe the key ingredient to a healthy church is that its mission and purpose be rooted in the Great Commission, and that is what matters the most.

When a man breathes his last breathe, his salvation will NOT be based upon whether or not he believes the shape of the Earth to flat. His salvation rests alone on his belief that Jesus Christ is God who came to Earth to live a perfect life, died on a cross, and after being dead and buried for three days was raised to life to defeat the grave. That is the gospel, the GOOD NEWS, and the reason our heart should beat for Christ and Christ alone every moment. We are forever grateful for the gift of salvation he offers us through his sacrifice.

The church I attend and serve at is healthy, and I am so very thankful to be apart of it. Would I ever leave the church on the sole premise that they chose to ignore and disregard the importance of the doctrine of the shape of the Earth that is completely Biblically based? No!

Do I wish they would stop printing on the church worship folder, and other materials, images of satanic icons of the Globe Earth with a cross on it and the words "Developing A Biblical Worldview" inscribed over top of that satanic Globe Earth icon? Yes!

Do I wish they would remove the NASA look-a-like images painted all throughout the hallways of the Children's Ministry area? Yes!

Do I wish they would stop printing Children's Ministry materials that push forward and further indoctrinate the minds of God's children with a satanically based Heliocentric Universe model? Yes!

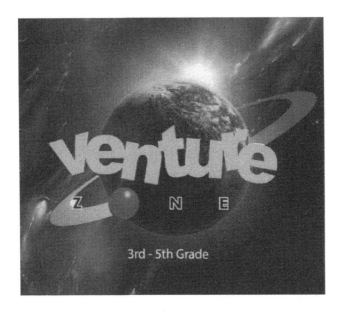

Do I wish they would stop planning their Vacation Bible School themes around a heretically based Heliocentric Universe model and putting stickers of cartoon planets all over the Children's Ministry's front desk to advertise VBS? Yes!

Do I wish they had not placed globular shaped NASA planets all throughout the Worship Center during VBS week, which danced over our heads during a Sunday service while the Pastor delivered his sermon message? Yes!

Do I wish they would stop giving the children pictures to color with a Globe Earth printed on it and the verse John 3:16 written out beside it? Yes!

Do I wish they would just adopt and teach the Biblically based doctrine of the shape of the Earth? Absolutely!

I pray the Lord will raise up more pastors like Dean Odle, Pastor of Fire & Grace Church located in Opelika, Alabama, who stand firmly on God's Word. Pastors who are bold enough to teach a Biblical doctrine like the Flat Earth despite it being extremely adverse to the common man's mindset. It is well past the time for true believers and followers of Jesus Christ to live a life that is actually different from the world's expectations and perspective. Christians need to abide in God's Word wholeheartedly. Yeshua, who will return one day named as Faithful and True (Rev. 19:11), please return soon!

CHAPTER 10: 216 "FLAT EARTH" BIBLE VERSES

I will never forget the time during a recent Christmas get together with some people from my side of the family. It was a lot of fun, except for when one of my relatives and I somehow started speaking about Flat Earth. As I insisted that the Bible proclaims the Flat Earth as truth, even more admittedly my relative stated otherwise. So, I conceded to stay away from Bible verses that reference the Earth as being stationary and flat, and, instead, only discuss observations and experiments that serve as a proof for Flat Earth the conversation continued towards a downward spiral. At that time my relative wanted nothing to do with the "ridiculousness of Flat Earth." I can't blame my relative for taking such a hard stance, cause I too experienced the same cognitive dissonance when Flat Earth was initially introduced to me.

As I have previously stated, it took me six months of intensive independent research, study, and experimentation to finally, let go of the cartoon Globe Earth and Planets that have been programmed into my mind throughout my entire life, and finally embrace the Biblical truth of Flat Earth. I have spoken with some who it took much less time to come around. I have also spoken with others who it has taken decades before they came around to the truth of a Biblically based Flat Earth.

I get it. Each man must receive this truth in his own time. It must not be forced upon others, as I know I have been guilty of doing so in the past. And, if you are someone I have attempted to force "Flat Earth" upon, please do forgive me.

If you are truly ready to embrace Flat Earth as a Biblically based doctrine or are at least interested in furthering your independent study, then you are in luck! I have compiled all 216 Bible verses used throughout this book that reference the Earth as being something other than a globular shaped Earth. In fact, I was unable to find even 1 verse that definitively conveys the Earth to be a globe-shaped object that spins on its axis and rotates around the Sun.

I have grouped these 216 Bible verses by 23 different themes. Lord willing, if it hasn't already happened by the time you read this, then these 216 Bible verses will soon be available on a t-shirt for you to wear at church events and family socials. Hopefully, the t-shirt will be used as a tool to encourage healthy and open discussion about the doctrine of the shape of the Earth. If you want one of these t-shirts, please email me at nathan@FlatEarthDoctrine.com.

In any case, here is the list of 216 Bible verses. Please, enjoy and be sure to share this list in truth and love with others, as they are willing to receive!

Earth Created Before the Sun: Genesis 1:1-19

Universe is Complete: Genesis 2:1

Earth Measurements Unknown: Job 38:4-5, Jeremiah 31:37, Proverbs 25:3

Earth is a Disk/Circle, not a ball: Isaiah 40:22, Job 38:13-14

Earth Measured with a Line, not a curve: Job 38:4-5

Paths are Straight, not curved: 1 Samuel 6:12, Psalm 5:8, Psalm 27:11, Isaiah 40:3, Jeremiah 31:9, Matthew 3:3, Mark 1:3, Luke 3:4, John 1:23, Acts 16:11, Acts 21:1, Hebrews 12:13

Waters are Straight, not curved: Job 37:10

Earthquakes shake Earth, and does not move: 2 Samuel 22:8, Isaiah 13:13, Revelation 6:12-13

Earth is fixed and immovable: Psalm 93:1, Psalm 96:10, Psalm 104:5, Psalm 119:89-90, Isaiah 45:18, 1 Chronicles 16:30

"Be still, and know that I am God": Psalm 46:10

Earth has Pillars, and hangs on nothing: 1 Samuel 2:8, Job 9:6, Job 26:7, Psalm 75:3, 2 Peter 3:5

Earth has a Face (a geometrical flat surface): Genesis 1:29, Genesis 4:14, Genesis 6:1, Genesis 6:7, Genesis 7:3, Genesis 7:4, Genesis 8:9, Genesis 11:8, Genesis 11:9, Genesis 41:56, Exodus 32:12, Exodus 33:16, Numbers 12:3, Deuteronomy 6:15, Deuteronomy 7:6, 1 Samuel 20:15, 1 Kings 13:34, Job 37:12, Psalm 104:30, Jeremiah 25:26, Jeremiah 28:16, Ezekiel 34:6, Ezekiel 38:20, Ezekiel 39:14, Amos 9:6, Amos 9:8, Zechariah 5:3

Waters have a Face (a geometrical flat surface): Genesis 1:2, Genesis 7:18, Job 38:30

Earth has Ends: Deuteronomy 28:49, Deuteronomy 28:64, Deuteronomy 33:17, 1 Samuel 2:10, Job 37:3, Job 38:13, Psalm 46:9, Psalm 48:10, Psalm 59:13, Psalm 61:2, Psalm 65:5, Psalm 67:7, Psalm 72:8, Psalm 98:3, Psalm 135:7, Proverbs 8:29, Proverbs 17:24, Proverbs 30:4, Isaiah 5:26, Isaiah 26:15, Isaiah 40:28, Isaiah 41:5, Isaiah 41:9, Isaiah 42:10, Isaiah 43:6, Isaiah 45:22, Isaiah 48:20, Isaiah 49:6, Isaiah 52:10, Jeremiah 10:13, Jeremiah 16:19, Jeremiah 25:31, Jeremiah 25:33, Jeremiah 51:16, Daniel 4:22, Micah 5:4, Zechariah 9:10, Acts 13:47

Earth has Corners: Isaiah 11:12, Revelation 7:1

Firmament/Dome: Genesis 1:6-8, Genesis 1:14-18, Genesis 1:20, Genesis 7:11, Genesis 8:2, Job 37:18,

Psalm 19:1, Psalm 150:1, Isaiah 40:22, Ezekiel 1:22-26, Ezekiel 10:1, Daniel 12:3

Sun Moves, not the Earth: Genesis 15:12, Genesis 15:17, Genesis 19:23, Genesis 32:31, Exodus 17:12, Exodus 22:3, Exodus 22:26, Leviticus 22:7, Numbers 2:3, Numbers 21:11, Numbers 34:15, Deuteronomy 4:41, Deuteronomy 4:47, Deuteronomy 11:30, Deuteronomy 16:6, Deuteronomy 23:11, Deuteronomy 24:13, Deuteronomy 24:15, Joshua 1:15, Joshua 8:29, Joshua 10:27, Joshua 12:1, Joshua 13:5, Joshua 19:12, Joshua 19:27, Joshua 19:34, Judges 8:13, Judges 9:33, Judges 14:18, Judges 19:14, Judges 20:43, 2 Samuel 2:24, 2 Samuel 3:35, 2 Samuel 23:4, 1 Kings 22:36, 2 Chronicles 18:34, Psalm 50:1, Psalm 113:3, Ecclesiastes 1:5, Isaiah 41:25, Isaiah 45:6, Isaiah 59:19, Jeremiah 15:9, Daniel 6:14, Amos 8:9, Jonah 4:8, Micah 3:6, Nahum 3:17, Malachi 1:11, Matthew 5:45, Mark 16:2, Ephesians 4:26, James 1:11

Sun STOPS moving: Isaiah 60:20, Job 9:7, Joshua 10:12-14, Habakkuk 3:11

Moon has its own Light: Genesis 1:16, Isaiah 13:10, Isaiah 30:26, Isaiah 60:19-20, Jeremiah 31:35, Matthew 24:29, Mark 13:24, Ezekiel 32:7, Revelation 21:23

High Altitude Perspectives: Daniel 4:11, Daniel 4:20, Matthew 4:8

Everyone Sees Jesus: Revelation 1:7

New Jerusalem, the HUGE cube: Revelation 21:15-17

Matthews Bible from 1537 says "Flat Earth": 2 Samuel 11:11

THANK YOU

This book is dedicated to Yeshua (aka Jesus), the Lord of lords and King of kings, who will return one day to establish his Kingdom upon His flat and immovable Earth.

"And I saw heaven opened, and behold a white horse, and he that sat upon him was called **Faithful and True**, and in righteousness he doth judge and make war." - Revelation 19:11 (RSB)

A special thank you to my wife and children for their patience with me as it took me several months to complete this work.

There have been many before me whose experiments, art, song, and research has inspired me to investigate the true shape of the Earth. I may not agree or share every belief with the following persons, regardless; each of the following persons has spoken the truth in one way or another, which has helped me along my journey to discovering what God's Word states about the shape of His Earth:

- Alexander Gleason (Author of "Is the Bible from Heaven? Is the Earth a Globe?" and creator of the 1892 azimuthal equidistant map)
- B.o.B. (Musician)
- Brian Mullin (Engineer)

- Caleb Waters (Researcher & Friend; aka NorCal Waters)
- David E. Robinson (Author of many books)
- David Wardlaw Scott (Author of "Terra Firma")
- Edward Hendrie (Attorney and Author of "The Greatest Lie on Earth")
- Eric Dubay (Author of many books)
- Jaba (Musician)
- Mark Sargent (Author of "Flat Earth Clues")
- Matt Boylan (Artist; aka Matthew Powerland)
- Matthew Henderson (Researcher & Friend)
- Rick Delano (Movie: "The Principle")
- Rob Skiba (Author of many books)
- Robbie Davidson (movie: Scientism Exposed)
- Robert Sungenis (movie: "The Principle")
- Samuel Birley Rowbotham (Author of "Zetetic Astronomy" and Inventor)
- William Carpenter (Author of "100 proofs that the Earth is not a globe")

Thank you to those who have permitted me to share your publically written testimony in this book to bear witness to the impact that the doctrine of the shape of the Earth has had upon your life.

A special thank you to Tina Baugh and Sydney Brunner for taking the time to providing input and feedback to help make this book more complete.

Thank you to Erik Brunner for his encouragement and support.

If you'd like to connect with me and continue to support my current and future work, feel free to do one or all of the following:

1. Like my Facebook page named "The Doctrine of the Shape of the Earth"

2. Email me at nathan@FlatEarthDoctrine.com

3. Follow me on Twitter @DocShapeOfEarth

4. Follow me on Amazon.com

5. Visit www.FlatEarthDoctrine.com

Endnotes

(a) https://youtu.be/_Xn3G7kx2A4

(b) https://mainerepublicmailalert.com; I also recommend you research this website too: www.understandcontractlawandyouwin.com

(c) https://en.wikipedia.org/wiki/Kola_Superdeep_Borehole

(d) https://en.wikipedia.org/wiki/Challenger_Deep

(e) https://www.space.com/11337-human-spaceflight-records-50th-anniversary.html

(f) http://www.euronews.com/2015/03/16/the-final-frontier-astronauts-on-iss-tell-euronews-about-humanity-s-future-in-

(g) https://earthobservatory.nasa.gov/Features/OrbitsCatalog/

(h) https://en.wikipedia.org/wiki/Seal_(emblem)

(i) https://youtu.be/YXmBzrS7bbQ

(j) https://savageplane.wordpress.com/tag/flat-earth/

(k) https://en.wikipedia.org/wiki/Lake_Baikal

(l) https://flatearthscienceandbible.com/2016/02/08/top-ten-undeniable-flat-earth-proofs/

(m) http://www.ats.aq/e/ats.htm

(n) https://youtu.be/KcxraxCQCd0

(o) http://faithofgod.net/tanak/2sa.htm#11:1

(p)http://www.ourhollowearth.com/ourhollo/index.
html;http://www.holloworbs.com/Etidor_william_
morgan.htm

Made in the USA
Columbia, SC
16 September 2019